Christians in a Secular Age

Mike Willis

Guardian of Truth Foundation
C E I Bookstore
220 S. Marion St. •Athens, AL 35611
1-855-492-6657

ISBN 10: 1-58427-399-2

ISBN 13: 978-1-58427-399-8

Guardian of Truth Foundation
C E I Bookstore
220 S. Marion St. • Athens, AL 35611
1-855-492-6657

Table of Contents

Before and After

Each lesson contains an activity entitled "Before and After." The question is designed to highlight the main theme of the lesson and see how the lesson contents affect your thoughts about the subject under discussion. Therefore, before you begin to read the lesson, do the "before" section of the question. After you have finished the lesson, go back and answer the same question again.

Introduction

There is a great spiritual war occurring in which every man is a soldier (Rev. 12:17; Eph. 6:10-18). The war has been going on since creation and the arch-enemy of mankind is Satan. He is relentless in his efforts to persuade man to disobey the Lord's will. Satan's success in persuading twenty-first century man to disobey God cannot be denied. As we witness the culture wars occurring in our homeland, we lament the success of the homosexual lobby groups, the widespread use of abortion as a means of birth control, sexual cohabitation outside of wedlock, the breakdown of the American family (and consequent poverty and crime), greed, materialism, political corruption, and other evidences of Satan's influence in our culture.

The Victory Belongs to Christ

However, we must never lose hope or become despondent. We know how this battle is going to end. King Jesus has already won the victory at the cross (Eph. 1:22-23; Col. 2:15). The book of Revelation pictures His defeat of the religio-political forces of the Roman empire as well as His ultimate victory over Satan and his minions in the following text:

> Now I saw heaven opened, and behold, a white horse. And He who sat on him was called Faithful and True, and in righteousness He judges and makes war. His eyes were like a flame of fire, and on His head were many crowns. He had a name written that no one knew except Himself. He was clothed with a robe dipped in blood, and His name is called The Word of God. And the armies in heaven, clothed in fine linen, white and clean, followed Him on white horses. Now out of His mouth goes a sharp sword, that with it He should strike the nations. And He Himself will rule them with a rod of iron. He Himself treads the winepress of the fierceness and wrath of Almighty God. And He has on His robe and on His thigh a name written: KING OF KINGS AND LORD OF LORDS. Then I saw an angel standing in the sun; and he cried with a loud voice, saying to all the birds that fly in the midst of heaven, "Come and gather together for the supper of the great God, that you may eat the flesh of kings, the flesh of captains, the flesh of mighty men, the flesh of horses and of those who sit on them, and the flesh of all people, free and slave, both small and great." And I saw the beast, the kings of the earth, and their armies, gathered together to make war against Him who sat on the horse and against His army. Then the beast was captured, and with him the false prophet who worked signs in his presence, by which he deceived those who received the mark of the beast and those who worshiped his image. These two were cast alive into the lake of fire burning with brimstone. And the rest were killed with the sword which proceeded from the mouth of Him who sat on the horse. And all the birds were filled with their flesh (Rev. 19:11-21).

The good news is that the victory belongs to Christ. Comparing Jesus' victory over sin and death to a Roman emperor leading his victorious soldiers and captives in a triumphal entrance into

Before and After	
Why do you believe the following is true or false?	
America is a Christian nation. Because we are Christians, God has given our nation a unique position, different from that of other nations. America is His instrument to spread Christian values in the world.	
Before	**After**

the city of Rome, Paul describes Jesus's triumph as follows:

> Now thanks be to God who always leads us in triumph in Christ, and through us diffuses the fragrance of His knowledge in every place. For we are to God the fragrance of Christ among those who are being saved and among those who are perishing. To the one we are the aroma of death leading to death, and to the other the aroma of life leading to life (2 Cor. 2:14-16).

As we begin this study of issues facing us at the beginning of the twenty-first century in America, it is important that we know what the outcome of this battle is going to be. Ultimately the victory belongs to the Lord. Regardless of the temporal circumstances of the period in which we live, we know that the victory belongs to Christ.

Satan Changes His Tactics

What Satan uses to deceive mankind in one age may not be what he uses in the next, although his temptations will always appeal to the lust of the eye, the lust of the flesh, and the pride of life (1 John 2:15-17). Whereas the truth of God is everlasting and does not change, Satan's lies change to deceive the most people in any given age. Therefore, the earthly conflict between the forces of good and evil are constantly in a state of flux and change. The nature of Satan's assault in one era may be completely different from his assault in another era, and, surprisingly, his old lies crop up anew in a later generation. To illustrate this, consider the changes that have occurred in denominationalism in the last 150 years: The teachings of the Protestant denominations of the late nineteenth and early twentieth centuries are significantly different from what is generally taught today. The nineteenth century Protestant denominations tenaciously adhered to their formal creeds espousing

the unique doctrines that separated one denomination from another. Every church was convinced that the doctrines that distinguished their church from other denominations were right and should be forcefully preached. The result was warring denominations; the church's reaction was ecumenism – unity without regard to doctrinal differences.

Today late twentieth and early twenty-first century Protestant denominations have only a historical connection with their formal creeds. Their members pay little attention to them and informed Christians know more about the creeds of the various Protestant churches than do their own members. The nineteenth and early twentieth century Protestant denominations did not defend abortion, receive homosexuals (and certainly did not allow homosexuals in the pulpit), allow easy divorce and remarriage, and generally preached the truth on a host of other moral issues. Nor did they generally question the deity of Christ, the miracles of the Bible, and the inspiration of Scripture. But these are common to late twentieth and early twenty-first century Protestant churches. Indeed, Satan has adjusted his deceitful message to win twenty-first century men.

Nationalism and American Exceptionalism

Inasmuch as we will be discussing issues related to what is sometimes called "culture wars" in America in the late twentieth and early twenty-first century, it is imperative that one distinguishes nationalism from Christianity. There is a large Baptist Church in our area that has an annual special event on July 4th. It has a fireworks display and preaches special "God and country" sermons. Because the gospel of Christ is wrapped in the American flag, the line

NOTES

_____
_____
_____
_____
_____
_____

between national patriotism and Christianity is blurred. One cannot tell where Christianity ends and national patriotism begins. When the gospel is preached in foreign countries, the evangelist is aware that he must be careful not to allow American cultural issues to interfere with the proclamation of God's word. The same carefulness is needed in preaching at home. To some Christians America is "God's country," as if it stands in some unique place in God's divine purpose. Indeed, our country looks upon itself as exceptional among all the nations on earth.[1]

The theory of *American exceptionalism* can be traced to Alexis de Tocqueville, the first writer to describe the United States as "exceptional" in 1831 and 1840.[2] The idea of American exceptionalism led to what historians call the doctrine of *manifest destiny*. The idea involves these three themes: (a) the virtue of the American people and their institutions; (b) the mission to spread these institutions, thereby redeeming and remaking the world in the image of the United States; (c) the destiny under God to do this work.[3] Religious people who believe in American exceptionalism and manifest destiny

act as if the United States occupies a special relationship with God that other governments do not have; it is the new Israel of God!

In all of human history, God selected only one nation with whom He entered into a special relationship – Israel (not the modern state of Israel but the biblical state). The prophet Malachi spoke of God's selection/election of Israel saying, "'I have loved you,' says the LORD. 'Yet you say, "In what way have You loved us?" Was not Esau Jacob's brother?' Says the LORD. Yet Jacob I have loved; But Esau I have hated, And laid waste his mountains and his heritage For the jackals of the wilderness" (Mal. 1:2-3).[4] God had chosen to make of the descendants of Abraham through Jacob a nation of people to whom He gave the land of Canaan (Gen. 12:1-3, 7) and entered a special relationship:

> For you are a holy people to the LORD your God; the LORD your God has chosen you to be a people for Himself, a special treasure above all the peoples on the face of the earth. The LORD did not set His love on you nor choose you because you were more in number than any other people, for you were the least of all peoples; but because the LORD loves you, and because He would keep the oath which He swore to your fathers, the LORD has brought you out with a mighty hand, and redeemed you from the house of bondage, from the hand of Pharaoh king of Egypt (Deut. 7:6-8; cf. 10:15; Isa. 41:8-9).

God never entered into such a relationship with any other nation of people. We err if we think that

---

[1] One should consider what attitudes a feeling of American exceptionalism might produce among its citizens. Are Americans better than others? Is America invulnerable to military assaults from those outside the nation? Is American culture superior to others? Is capitalism the only economic system authorized by God?

[2] Alexia de Tocqueville, *Democracy in America* (1840), part 2, page 36: "The position of the Americans is therefore quite exceptional, and it may be believed that no other democratic people will ever be placed in a similar one" (*http://en.wikipedia.org/wiki/American_ exceptionalism*, accessed 2/21/2014).

[3] See *http://en.wikipedia.org/wiki/Manifest_Destiny* (accessed 2/20/2014).

---

[4] Malachi is not speaking of the election/reprobation of Jacob/Esau as recipients of eternal salvation/ damnation. Jacob and Esau were the primogenitures of their respective nations – Israel and Edom. The election under discussion is God's choice to enter a special covenant with the descendants of Jacob (Israel) and not with the descendants of Esau (Edom).

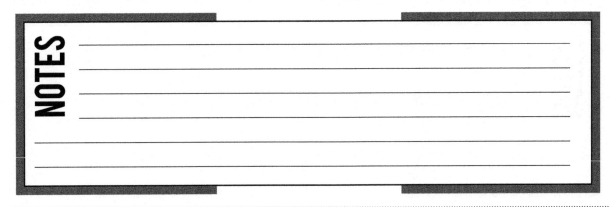

NOTES

He has such a relationship with our own or any other modern nation!

Because the Jewish nation rejected God's Messiah (Christ), He terminated this unique relationship with the nation of Israel. Israel's unbelief caused Jesus to say, "Therefore I say to you, the kingdom of God will be taken from you and given to a nation bearing the fruits of it" (Matt. 21:43). Jesus pronounced God's judgment against Israel in His prophecy of the destruction of Jerusalem (Matt. 24; Mark 13; Luke 21). The descriptions that had been applied to Israel's special covenant relationship with God now are applied to the church, not to a political nation (see Exod. 19:5-6; 1 Pet. 2:5-9).

The Scriptures teach that God is sovereign over the nations. Paul said, "And He has made from one blood every nation of men to dwell on all the face of the earth, and *has determined their preappointed times and the boundaries of their dwellings*" (Acts 17:26). He was preaching what the prophets of Israel had proclaimed. In explaining Nebuchadnezzar's dream, Daniel said, "Blessed be the name of God forever and ever, For wisdom and might are His. And He changes the times and the seasons; *He removes kings and raises up kings*..." (Dan. 2:20-21). God's sovereignty was not limited to Israel; rather it included all the nations of the earth (1 Chron. 29:30; Psa. 75:6-7; Jer. 27:5). Proud Nebuchadnezzar who boasted that he had built Babylon (Dan. 4:30) thought that his position came because of his own wisdom and strength. He was placed under a divine judgment "that the living may know that *the Most High rules in the kingdom of men, Gives it to whomever He will*, and setteth up over it the basest of men" (Dan. 4:17, 25, 32). Daniel saw God's hand in Nebuchadnezzar's rise to power (Dan. 5:18, 19). The same God who raised him to power later brought judgment against the Babylonian kingdom when it was weighed in the balances and found wanting (Dan. 5:27).

The hand of God raised up the Assyrians whom He used as the rod of divine anger to punish Israel (Isa. 10:5). He raised up Babylon to bring judgment against Judah, in a judgment that astounded God's people because a nation more wicked than Judah was used to punish God's chosen people (Hab. 1:5-13). In the Biblical record through the millennia, God raised up Assyrian, Babylonian, Persian, Grecian, Ptolemaic, Seleucid, and Roman empires who ruled the world prior to the coming of Christ. Because the Bible was completed and new revelation has ceased to be given, man cannot specifically identify God's actions as sovereign ruler over the nations since that time. But in the two thousand years since His Son died on Calvary, many powerful nations have had their day in the sun and subsequently faded into oblivion in God's providential governance of the world. What has happened with other powerful nations is happening with our own beloved country.

The basis for God's sovereign rule over the nations is succinctly stated: "Righteousness exalts a nation, But sin is a reproach to any people" (Prov. 14:34).[5] Jeremiah expressed God's dealings with the nations in the following prophecy:

"O house of Israel, can I not do with you as this potter?" says the LORD. "Look, as the clay is in the potter's hand, so are you in My hand, O house of Israel! The instant I speak concerning a nation and concerning a kingdom, to pluck

---

[5] God's righteous governance of the world is seen in the destruction of Sodom and Gomorrah and the cities of the Plain (Gen. 19) as well as in the universal flood (Gen. 6-8).

NOTES

_____
_____
_____
_____
_____
_____

up, to pull down, and to destroy it, if that nation against whom I have spoken turns from its evil, I will relent of the disaster that I thought to bring upon it. And the instant I speak concerning a nation and concerning a kingdom, to build and to plant it, if it does evil in My sight so that it does not obey My voice, then I will relent concerning the good with which I said I would benefit it" (Jer. 18:6-10).

Israel's prosperity was dependent upon her obedience to the Lord (see Deut. 28-29). God preserved a righteous remnant of Israel in order to accomplish His purposes in bringing the Messiah into the world. But that was not true for other nations. Where are the remnants of the Hittites, Amorites, Moabites, Jebusites, etc.? As painful as it may be for patriotic Americans to think in such terms, the fact remains that God's principles of the moral government of the world apply to our United States just as certainly as they have to all other nations of people. God is not bound to a covenant to save a remnant of Americans and restore the former glory of our kingdom.

Is America Christian?

The word "Christian" is only used as a noun and that in three passages in the Bible (Acts 11:26; 26:28; 1 Pet. 4:16). In each of these passages, the word is applied to individuals. It is used to describe those people who have believed in the Lord Jesus, repented of their sins, confessed their faith in Him, and been immersed (baptized) in water for the remission of their sins (Acts 2:37-38; 8:37-38). The word "Christian" is never used in Scripture to refer to a business, school, publication, missionary agency, town, state, or nation! In this sense, America never was and never could have been Christian! If it cannot be baptized, it cannot be a Christian!

However, in modern parlance, the word "Christian" is used as an adjective. It is frequently used as an adjective with these meanings: (a) "of, pertaining to, or derived from Jesus Christ or His teaching" (a Christian faith); (b) of, pertaining to, believing in, or belonging to the religion based on the teachings of Jesus Christ" (Spain is a Christian country) (c) "of or pertaining to Christians" (many Christian deaths in the Crusades) (d) "exhibiting a spirit proper to a follower of Jesus Christ; Christlike" (She displayed true Christian charity); (e) "decent; respectable" (They gave him a good Christian burial).[6]

We sometimes speak of America being a Christian nation in sense (b) above. By this we mean "that the vast majority of the people believe in Christ and the gospel, that Christian influences are universal, and that the civilization and intellectual culture are built on that foundation."[7] In this use of the English word, there was a time when America could be called a Christian nation.

But majorities change over time, as has been the case throughout human history.[8] Sometimes Israel was faithful to the Lord and at other times they apostatized into idolatry and immorality. What was true of Israel is true of all nations – nations are never constant. Righteous nations can become unrighteous and unrighteous nations can become righteous. In more recent years, America has made a consistent move

---

[6] *http://dictionary.reference.com/browse/christian*.

[7] Michael Babcock, *Unchristian America*, 49.

[8] The book of Judges laments the time relatively soon after the conquest of Canaan when "there arose another generation after them, which knew not the LORD, nor yet the works which he had done for Israel" (2:10). Just as this change occurred in Israel, so also is it now occurring in our own country.

NOTES
_____
_____
_____
_____
_____
_____
_____

away from Christian beliefs and values to those based on secular thought.[9]

Conclusion

Our beloved country has no unique relationship with God that makes it exceptional. It is just like all other nations. America will be blessed or cursed depending upon its righteous-

---

[9] Secularism may be described by several names: materialism, naturalism, humanism, or atheism.

ness or unrighteousness (Jer. 18:6-10). My generation has lived through a transition from a broadly based Christian value system to a predominantly secular value system that is destroying the family, devaluing life, and debasing our culture. The secular value system that has replaced Christianity in America will be what is studied. Regardless of what becomes of our nation, Christians know that the victory has already been secured through the resurrection of Christ.

Questions

1. What is Christ's purpose in informing Christians of the outcome of the present spiritual battle from the beginning (Rev. 19:11-21)?_____

2. What changes can you identify in how Satan assaults mankind in the following areas:

   a. The allurement of denominationalism?_____

   b. Sensual temptations? _____

   c. His use of TV, music, movies, and other media? _____

   d. Assaults on the family? _____

3. Why is it dangerous to allow American values to be equated with divine commands? _____
   _____

4. What made Israel's national relationship with God unique among the nations?_____
   _____

5. Why did God enter a unique relationship with Israel?_____
   _____

6. When did this relationship end and why? _____
   _____

7. What does it mean to say that "God is sovereign over the nations"? _____
   _____

8. How does God raise up and debase the kingdoms of men? _____
   _____

9. What principle governs the rise and fall of kingdoms (Prov. 14:34)? _____
   _____

10. In what sense are both of the following true?

    a. "America never has been and never can be Christian"?_____
    _____

    b. "American was a Christian nation"? _____
    _____

The Prevailing Non-Christian Worldview

Eric Hedin is an Assistant Professor in the Department of Physics and Astronomy at Ball State University in Muncie, IN. He taught a course in 2013 called "The Boundaries of Science" which, according to University of Chicago ecology professor Jerry A. Coyne, "was heavily loaded with Intelligent Design, Christian apologetics, and no counteracting views." Coyne contacted Ball State University officials about the matter, but did not get any action from them, so he contacted the Freedom From Religion Foundation and notified them that this was a potential violation of the First Amendment. They took it from there. Ball State University President Jo Ann Gora later announced that Prof. Hedin would not be fired but that he could no longer teach his class on "The Boundaries of Science." Apparently academic freedom does not include the right to present a view that questions evolutionary theory.[1]

Jack C. Phillips, co-owner of Masterpiece Cakeshop in Denver, in July 2012 told Charlie Craig and David Mullins that he would not bake a cake for their wedding. He said, as a long-practicing Christian, he believed God intended marriage to be for one man and one woman.

---

[1] Seth Slabaugh, *The (Muncie, IN) Star Press* (May 21, 2013), *http://www.usatoday.com/story/news/nation/2013/05/21/ball-state-professor-creationism-science-class/2345511/*, accessed 2/21/2014.

He also told the couple, "I'll make you birthday cakes, shower cakes, sell you cookies and brownies, I just don't make cakes for same-sex weddings." He believed he was protected in this because the Colorado Constitution defined marriage as between one man and one woman. However, Colorado administrative law judge, Robert N. Spencer, ordered Phillips to "cease and desist" his practice. He ruled that a private business doesn't have a right to refuse service to anyone it chooses.[2]

Complaints and lawsuits occur each Christmas season by groups that try to force cities and towns to remove their annual nativity scenes. Homosexual lovers are given the most attractive roles in nearly every sit-com, whereas Christian leaders who object to homosexuality are consistently portrayed in a negative light. Violence unlike what any of us remember in our youth is steadily increasing in America. The

---

[2] Dennis Byrne, "Half-baked decision on same-sex wedding cake," *http://articles.chicagotribune.com/2013-12-17/opinion/ct-oped-byrne-1217-20131217_1_wedding-cake-masterpiece-cakeshop-charlie-craig*, accessed 2/21/2014. A similar case in Oregon had similar results (*http://www.deseretnews.com/article/865595058/Oregon-will-oversee-settlement-process-between-Christian-bakers-lesbian-couple.html?pg=all*, accessed 2/21/2014).

Before and After	
Why are such incidences as the following hypothetical situation occurring?	
The local school district was sued by the Freedom From Religion Foundation because the basketball team began each game with a prayer?	
Before	**After**

TV programs constantly push the envelope to remove limits on whatever sexual promiscuity or profanity can be aired. Fornication is used to entertain its audience and only the most prudish parent would expect that his teenager maintain his sexual purity until marriage.

Christians who witness such incidents as cited above are troubled over the direction that American society is headed. What has changed in our society that we have such things occurring? There is not one answer to this question; there are many contributing factors. However, one predominant theme stands out and is the subject of this workbook. A worldview that rejects Christianity now controls the media, education, and political institutions of America.

In this lesson, we will present an overview of this worldview and how it differs from Christianity. The very briefest of historical information will be presented to trace its rise to power in America and then we will look at the worldview itself.

Historical Background

The new worldview in America goes under various names. It may be called secularism, materialism, naturalism, humanism, or atheism. Its roots go back several centuries.[3] In its earliest form, humanism was motivated by the desire to have literary knowledge and linguistic skills; early humanists would not have thought themselves opposed to Christianity. A split began to occur between the humanists and religion about the time that Galileo (1564-1642) began to advocate the Copernican theory that the earth revolves around the sun; at that time the Roman Catholic Church defended the idea that the earth was the

center of the universe. In the nineteenth century, the French Revolution established a society based on human reason alone.[4] In the 1930s, the signatories of the *Humanist Manifesto I* saw humanism as the religion of the future.

Humanism has had a tremendous influence in religious studies. In the nineteenth century a seminal work by David Friedrich Strauss (1808-1874) entitled *The Life of Jesus Critically Examined* eliminated the miraculous from His life.[5] The work suggested natural explanations for Jesus's "miracles." Strauss's work was a serious challenge to belief in the deity of Christ. The naturalistic explanation of Jesus and the Bible is that there are no miracles; the Biblical miracles are myths and legends and should be treated as non-historical. The atheist denies the existence of God; the deist believes God created the world, wound it up like a clock, and then allows it to run down without any outside intrusion. In either case, God is not involved in His creation, either because there is no god or that God does not interfere in earthly affairs. The implications of their beliefs for the inspiration of Scripture, the biblical history of Israel, and the deity of Christ are obvious.

Charles Darwin's (1809-1882) idea of evolution affected many branches of study, because it provided an explanation for life without the belief in God.[6] Evolutionary theory

[3] Francesco Petrarca (1304-1374) is often called the "Father of Humanism" (*http://en.wikipedia.org/wiki/Petrarch*, accessed 2/24/2014).

[4] Some of their critics referred to humanism as a cult that resulted in the "deification of humanity."

[5] Strauss argued, "Indeed no just notion of the true nature of history is possible, without a perception of the inviolability of the chain of finite causes, and of the impossibility of miracles" (74).

[6] It should be noted that early evolutionists were not atheistic and, even today, many are theistic evolutionists who believe God directed evolution over long periods of time. However, naturalistic evolution

NOTES
_____
_____
_____
_____
_____
_____

shaped religious studies by positing the evolutionary development of religion. The idea was that man's religious beliefs evolved through these stages: primitive religions (animism, totemism, etc.), polytheism (gods ascribed to each of the powers of nature), henotheism (the worship of a single god even though one admits the existence of others), monotheism, and finally Christianity, the highest expression of religion. Early evolutionary theorists thought Christianity was the highest development of religion. Since then, however, two changes have occurred: (a) humanists and atheists now believe that humanism/atheism is the highest development of religion; (b) post-modernists teach that, since there are no objective standards to measure religion, there is no basis for determining the superiority of any religion. All religions are equally right/wrong. Twenty-first century humanists believe religion is responsible for many of the evils of the world and would best be eliminated.[7]

Prominent humanists took control of the education system. Humanists, such as John Dewey (1859-1952), argued that education and learning are social and interactive processes, and thus the school itself is a social institution through which social reform can and should take place. Under the control of humanists, the

schools fostered further development of humanist values, including evolutionary theory (with its attendant doctrine of man), sex education (taught from the humanist perspective), and moral values (situational ethics, values clarification, relative truth). If not completely, then predominantly, the educational system in America is dominated by secularism. Controlling our children from pre-school through post graduate studies, humanist educators use the classroom to indoctrinate/propagandize our children with secular values (more will be said about this in Chapter 10).

Contrasting Secularism and Christianity

Let's now contrast secularism (humanism, materialism, naturalism, post-modernism) and Christianity (see chart on p.14).

1. God. Humanist Paul Kurtz wrote, "… we find that traditional views of the existence of God either are meaningless, have not yet been demonstrated to be true, or are tyrannically exploitative."[8] Secular humanists are agnostics, atheists, rationalists, or skeptics. The Christian view assumes the existence of God and believes that God's existence is evidenced through the things He has made (Acts 14:15-17; Rom. 1:18-22).

2. Origin of the universe. "Religious humanists regard the universe as self-existing and not created."[9] Most of the pagan religions that have left documents show doctrinal beliefs in a creation myth. The creation myth of humanists

---

eliminates God altogether and hypothesizes the big bang theory.

[7] Traditional religions are said to "inhibit humans from helping themselves or experience their full potentialities" and "encourage dependence rather than independence." "Promises of immortal salvation or fear of eternal damnation are both illusory and harmful" (*http://americanhumanist.org/Humanism/Humanist_Manifesto_II*, accessed 2/25/2014). Paul Kurtz wrote, "These religious activists not only are responsible for much of the terror and violence in the world today but stand in the way of solutions to the world's most serious problems" (*A Secular Humanist Declaration*, 9).

---

[8] Paul Kurtz, *A Secular Humanist Declaration*, 18.

[9] *Humanist Manifesto I* (1933). Available at *http://americanhumanist.org/Humanism/Humanist_Manifesto_I*, accessed 2/25/2014.

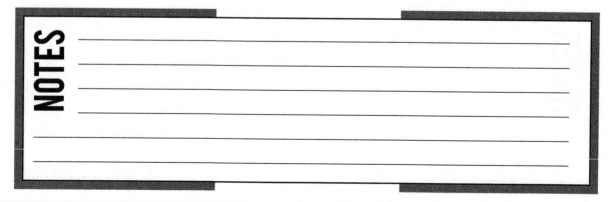

NOTES

Naturalism and Christianity Compared

SUBJECT	NATURALISM, SECULARISM	CHRISTIANITY
God	No deity or spirit world	Jehovah: Father, Son, and Holy Spirit
Origin	Creation Myth: The Big Bang Theory	Creation: Gen. 1-2
Man	Product of billions of years of undirected, chance evolution	Created in the image of God
Thought	The product of chance collision of molecules	The product of the soul created in the image of God
Will	The inevitable product of one's environment	Though influenced by environment and peers, man has free-will
History	Has no guiding hand and no purpose or end	Human history is controlled by God and has a divine purpose
Bible	The product of fallible men searching for a non-existent god	God's revelation of His will to man
Miracles	Have never occurred	Have occurred through the power of God
Jesus	A first century, illegitimate peasant who was a good moral teacher	The incarnate Son of God
Morals	There is no absolute truth; all moral judgments are relative	Moral values are revealed to God in Scripture and are absolute
Eschatology: Universal	When the solar system collapses, the entire universe will be destroyed	Earth will be destroyed when God wills it to occur
Eschatology: Personal	When man dies, there is no part of him that continues to exist; there is no judgment	At death, the body dies but the soul continues to exist; later the body will be raised and reunited with his spirit; man will be judged; eternal life or eternal damnation

NOTES

_____
_____
_____
_____
_____

is the "big bang theory."[10] The Bible teaches that God created the world (Gen. 1-2; Heb. 11:3).

3. Man. According to humanism, man is the product of unguided evolution.[11] Naturalists have to explain man without supernatural forces acting. Therefore, life itself must be explained as living matter evolving from non-living matter; speech evolved naturally (although there is no documented evidence of a primitive-to-modern speech evolution; all ancient languages are fully developed). Man is no different from any other animal, according to naturalists, although no other animal has written its own history (e.g., "The History of Dogs" by Fido). In contrast to naturalism, the Bible teaches that man is created in God's image and is given the role of ruler over His creation (Gen. 1:26-28; cf. Ps. 8).

4. Thought. According to naturalism, human thought is the product of the chance collision of molecules. Thought is the product of nerve functions (such as occurs when a piece of flesh touches a hot stove). But man not only thinks, he also has a conscience, which is unique to man. (Did you ever see a lion feeling guilty for eating a deer or a cat crying for having eaten a mouse?) Conscience assesses what has been done and gives either approval or disapproval of the behavior. It is more than a nerve reacting to burning stove. Naturalists reject the idea of a soul within the body.

5. Will. Again, naturalists must explain human will without involving the human soul. The result is that one's will is just the inevitable result of one's environment. Man is fatalistically determined to act a certain way by the environment in which he exists.[12] Whereas the Bible acknowledges the influence of environment and one's peers on human action, nevertheless man has free will to choose what he wishes to do (Josh. 24:15) and will be held accountable for his actions (2 Cor. 5:10).

6. History. For humanists, history has no purpose.[13] Whatever purpose is seen in human history is man injecting his subjective interpretation to a series of chance events. There is no objective history; in writing history man subjectively arranges selected events to tell a story of his own creation (indeed, history and fiction are very close to each other). There is no goal to human history. In contrast, the Biblical

---

[10] "According to the theory, the Big Bang occurred approximately 13.798 ± 0.037 billion years ago, which is thus considered the age of the universe. At this time, the universe was in an extremely hot and dense state and began expanding rapidly. After the initial expansion, the universe cooled sufficiently to allow energy to be converted into various subatomic particles, including protons, neutrons, and electrons. Though simple atomic nuclei formed within the first three minutes after the Big Bang, thousands of years passed before the first electrically neutral atoms formed. The majority of atoms that were produced by the Big Bang are hydrogen, along with helium and traces of lithium. Giant clouds of these primordial elements later coalesced through gravity to form stars and galaxies, and the heavier elements were synthesized either within stars or during supernovae" (*en.wikipedia.org/wiki/Big_Bang*, accessed 2/25/2014).

[11] "Humans are an integral part of nature, the result of unguided evolutionary change" (*http://americanhumanist.org/Humanism/Humanist_Manifesto_III*, accessed 2/25/2014).

[12] Think of criminal defenses that appeal to environment as the cause of the crime ("he was poor," "he was abused as a child," "he was uneducated," "he was raised in a racist environment") and argue that the criminal should not be held accountable on that basis.

[13] "But we can discover no divine purpose or providence for the human species" (*http://americanhumanist.org/Humanism/Humanist_Manifesto_II*, accessed 2/25/2014).

NOTES

_____
_____
_____
_____
_____
_____

narrative describes God creating the earth and mankind with a distinct goal in mind. All of human history is headed toward that final eschatological goal. He also controls all that happens between these two events. God is the God of history who has acted and continues to act in human history, as the Sovereign over His creation. He raises up and destroys nations according to His divine purpose and will (Dan. 4:25, 32).

7. The Bible. The humanist/naturalist/secularist view of the Bible is that it is of human origin. Denying the existence of God and, consequently, miracles (including divine revelation), the humanist explains the Bible as man's religious experiences, his efforts to explain the forces of nature that he does not understand, his efforts to establish a relationship with a non-existing God, and his efforts to impose moral imperatives that were traditional beliefs from an earlier period of human evolution. The Christian view of the Bible is that it is a divine revelation of God's will to mankind (2 Tim. 3:16-17; 1 Cor. 2:8-16; 2 Pet. 1:20-21).

8. Miracles. The denial of a divine being necessarily eliminates the miraculous. Stories of miracles are superstitions, legends, and myths invented for various reasons by those who told them. The Biblical view of miracles is that they manifest the power of God and had the purpose of providing evidence that God's divine will was being revealed by His chosen spokesman (John 3:2; 14:10-11; 20:30-31; Acts 2:22; 10:38; Heb. 2:4).

9. Jesus. The Jesus of naturalism is not the same as the Jesus of the Bible. Secularists believe that Jesus was the illegitimate son of Joseph and Mary, that He performed no miracles (therefore, He was like the modern faith healer or exorcist), He died on the cross in Jerusalem,

and His body rotted in a tomb. He could not save Himself from the cross and cannot save anyone else. Even humanists must admit that Jesus lived and was a good teacher of moral values. The Biblical doctrine of Jesus is that He was fully man (Jesus called Himself the "Son of Man" on many occasions; for examples see Matt. 8:20; 9:6; 10:23; 11:19; 12:8, 32, 40; 16:13; etc.) and fully God (called the "Son of God" on many occasions; see Matt. 4:3, 6; 8:29; 14:33; 26:53; John 1:34, 49; 3:18; 5:25; 9:35; 10:36; etc.). He alone can save man from his sins (Matt. 1:21; Luke 2:11; John 4:42; Acts 5:31; 13:23; Eph. 5:23; etc.).

10. Morals. The *Humanist Manifesto II* says, "We affirm that moral values derive their source from human experience. Ethics is autonomous and situational needing no theological or ideological sanction."[14] Paul Kurtz wrote,

> Morality that is not God-based need not be antisocial, subjective, or promiscuous, nor need it lead to the breakdown of moral standards. Although we believe in tolerating diverse lifesystles and social manners, we do not think they are immune to criticism. Nor do we believe that any one church should impose its views of moral virtue and sin, sexual conduct, marriage, divorce, birth control, or abortion, or legislate them for the rest of society.[15]

The Biblical view of morals is that God determines what is right and wrong and has revealed that to mankind, at first through His prophets and then through the Bible. Sin is the transgression of divine law (1 John 3:4) and unrighteousness (1 John 5:17).

---

[14] *Humanist Manifest II, http://americanhumanist. org/Humanism/Humanist_Manifesto_II*, accessed 2/25/2014.

[15] *A Secular Humanist Declaration*, 15.

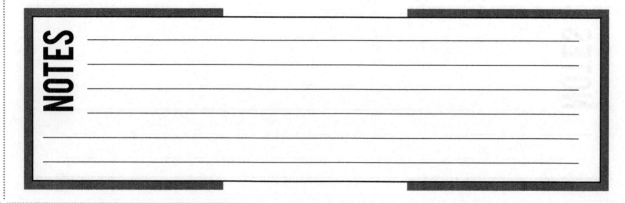

NOTES

11. Universal Eschatology. In the secular view, the universe will eventually be destroyed when gravity causes the universe to collapse on itself. Secularists are worried about the threat of global warming, nuclear holocaust, and population explosions that severely affect earthlife. However, "Promises of immortal salvation or fear of eternal damnation are both illusory and harmful."[16] In contrast, the Bible clearly teaches that the earth and universe will pass away (2 Pet. 3:9; Psa. 102:26), it will be followed by an eternal judgment (Heb. 9:27) leading to either eternal punishment or eternal life (Matt. 25:46).

12. Personal Eschatology. What happens to man when he dies? The secularist believes that man ceases to exist at death saying, "There is no credible evidence that life survives the death of the body."[17] For the humanist, death is the end of human existence. There is no judgment and no fear of hell or hope of heaven. In contrast, the Christian view is that the human spirit, which is made in the image of God, goes back to God at death (Eccl. 12:7). It goes to the Hadean world where it awaits judgment and either eternal life (Heaven) or eternal damnation (Hell) (Luke 16:19-31; Rev. 20:12-15; 21:8).

---

[16] *Humanist Manifesto II, http://americanhumanist. org/Humanism/Humanist_Manifesto_II*, accessed 2/25/2014.

---

[17] *Ibid.*

Questions

1. List some changes in American life that reflect a change in worldview in our society. _____
   _____

2. On the following topics, describe the prevailing politically correct worldview in America and provide a Scripture that shows the Christian worldview on the same topic.

   a. God_____

   b. Origin of the universe _____

   c. Man_____

   d. Thought _____

   e. Will _____

   f. History _____

   g. Bible _____

   h. Miracles _____

   i. Jesus _____

NOTES
_____
_____
_____
_____
_____
_____

j. Morals_____

k. Universal eschatology _____

l. Personal eschatology _____

3. What evidences of the non-Christian worldview do you see in ...

   a. TV presentations on the Bible narrative _____

   b. School books discussing human origins_____

   c. Morals_____

   d. Funerals _____

4. How does an awareness of this worldview and its control of the schools affect your understanding of why so many Christians have unbelieving children? _____

   _____

NOTES
_____
_____
_____
_____
_____
_____

Pluralism in America

One of the terms used frequently to describe American culture is "pluralism." In its basic definition, pluralism is (a) "a situation in which people of different social classes, religions, races, etc., are together in a society but continue to have their different traditions and interests" and (b) "the belief that people of different social classes, religions, races, etc., should live together in a society."[1] In both of these definitions, one cannot doubt that pluralism exists and is a part of modern American culture.

Kinds of Pluralism

D. A. Carson breaks pluralism down into three helpful categories:

1. Emperical pluralism. This refers to the undeniable fact that America has ethnic diversity, races, and social classes. Immigration patterns have brought people from widely different backgrounds to our country. Hindus and Buddhists have moved to the West; Hispanics have moved into neighborhoods all over America; Islamists have settled throughout America. This same emperical pluralism has occurred in most countries of the Western World. Diversity is becoming more common than a homogeneous population.

2. Cherished pluralism. This pluralism is distinguished from emperical pluralism by the addition of the idea of approval. Plurality is celebrated as something that is good for society. The media and intellectuals of the West celebrate cultural pluralism as enhancing American life.

3. Philosphical pluralism. This term is an umbrella term that encompasses a number of different positions but they are all, as Carson explains, "united in their opposition to the idea that we can know objective truth." Their stance is "that any notion that a particular ideological or religious claim is intrinsically superior to another is *necessarily* wrong."[2]

Philosophical pluralism is what this lesson is analyzing. Philosophical pluralism has developed because radical hermeneutics emphasize the subjective nature of all interpretation. The emphasis on the subjective nature of all interpretation resulted in the coining of the term "new hermeneutic" (later this term was replaced by "radical hermeneutics") to distinguish itself from an older hermeneutic that believed that there is an objective truth that can be known.[3]

---

[1] *http://www.merriam-webster.com/dictionary/pluralism*, accessed 2/26/2014.

[2] See D.A. Carson, *The Gagging of God*, pp. 12-19.

[3] Even modernists believed in the objectivity of

Before and After	
What is your reaction to the following situation?	
Americans should be thankful for the many churches because this enables individuals to find a church that fits their individual needs.	
Before	**After**

In post-modern thought, the idea of an objective truth that can be known has been replaced by the idea that all knowledge is colored by influences of one's social environment. Post-modernism has so affected our culture that 66% strongly agree or agree somewhat with the assertion that "there is no such thing as absolute truth."[4] The denial of absolute truth affects religion, morals, history, and all other departments of learning.

How Pluralism Affects Religious Studies

The basic tenet of pluralism is popularly expressed in such phrases as "all religions are really saying the same thing" or "all achieve salvation (whatever that means for the particular group) with equal efficiency." Philosophical pluralism leads to these conclusions: (a) No one religion can claim superiority to any other religion; (b) God has revealed Himself in other religions as well as Christianity; (c) The idea that all religions have some truth. When a religion disagrees with Christianity, each religion is equally valid for its own community. According to pluralism and post-modernism, an approach to world religion which views Christianity as superior to other religions is bigoted fundamentalism.

_____

knowledge and that the human mind can uncover such knowledge. However, post-modernists do not believe that there is an objective truth and, if there were, that it could be known. The self-contradiction of post-modernism is their absolute denial of objective truth. They absolutely know that there is no absolute truth!

[4] "One-third of all adults (34%) believe that moral truth is absolute and unaffected by the circumstances. Slightly less than half of the born again adults (46%) believe in absolute moral truth" (*https://www.bama.org/barna-update/21-transformation/252-barna-survey-examines-changes-in-worldview-among-christians-over-the-past-13-years#.Uw308YVnjdY*, accessed 2/26/2014).

Carson observes the impact of pluralism on Evangelical preaching saying, "It is hard, for instance, to deny the influence of pluralism on evangelical preachers who increasingly reconstruct the 'gospel' along the lines of felt needs, knowing that such a presentation will be far better appreciated than one that articulates truth with hard edges (i.e., that insists that certain contrary things are false), or that warns of the wrath to come."[5]

Christianity Was Born in a Pluralistic Society

One of the most impressive buildings that has survived from ancient times is located in the heart of Rome. It is known as the Pantheon. The word *Pantheon* is a Greek word made up of the word *pan* (all) and *Theos* (god); the Pantheon was a temple to all gods. The Temple was erected during the reign of Augustus Caesar by Marcus Agrippa in 27 B.C. during his third consulship. Roman society tried to unite its empire through incorporating the local deities of conquered people into its hierarchy of gods. The Greek gods were combined with the Roman gods, by recognizing that the gods of Greek and Rome only wore different names.[6]

Jews created a problem for Roman policy because they refused to allow Roman gods to be placed in the Temple at Jerusalem. The Old Testament clearly taught monotheism in a text often recited by the Jew which is called the Shema from the first word of the Hebrew text: "Hear, O Israel: The Lord our God is One Lord" (Deut. 6:4). The Ten Commandments forbade the

_____

[5] Carson, *op. cit.*, 30.

[6] See *http://ancienthistory.about.com/od/romangods/a/022709RomanGrk.htm* for a table of the Roman and Greek gods and goddesses.

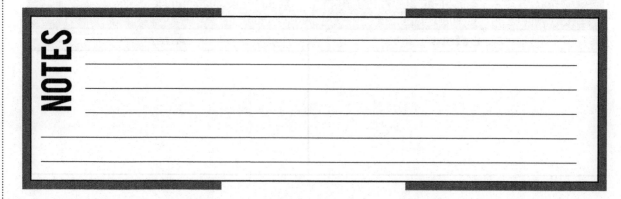

NOTES

worship of any other gods and forbade graven images (Exod. 20:2-4). Rome made special concession to allow Jews to worship in their own way without interference from the Caesars.[7] The threat of Jewish rebellion was exacerbated by Caligula's (A.D. 37-41) demand that his statue should be set up in the Temple.[8]

In the backdrop of the conflict between Romans and Jews, Christianity was born. The prevailing cultural was a pluralistic society. One can see how first-century Christians reacted to the pluralism of their day for guidance on how twenty-first century Christians should be reacting to the pluralism of our own age.

---

[7] See Josephus, *Antiquity of the Jews* XVI.x for a record of some of the concessions given to the Jews.

[8] *Ibid., XIX.i.1*

The Bible and Pluralism

First, one should notice that the Bible affirms that there is an objective truth that can and must be known in order to have eternal salvation. Jesus said, "And you shall know the truth, and the truth shall make you free" (John 8:32). Notice these conclusions from Jesus's statement: (a) There is an objective truth; (b) It can be known; (c) To be free from the bondage of sin, one must know that truth.

Truth is not discovered by human reason. Paul said, "For since, in the wisdom of God, the world through wisdom did not know God, it pleased God through the foolishness of the message preached to save those who believe" (1 Cor. 1:21). Paul did not preach man's wisdom but a divinely revealed word from God (1 Cor. 2:1-16). Truth is, therefore, grounded in God's revelation

The Pantheon was a temple to all gods. The Temple was erected during the reign of Augustus Caesar by Marcus Agrippa in 27 B.C. during his third consulship.

of His will to mankind. Jesus said it simply, "Thy (God's) word is truth" (John 17:17; cf. Psa. 119:142, 151).

Second, in the Old Testament, God rejected the worship of other gods (Exod. 20:3; Deut. 5:7; 6:14-15; 2 Kings 17:35; Jer. 25:6; 35:15). Not even God Himself could be worshiped with idols (Exod. 20:4; Lev. 26:1; Deut. 4:15-19; 5:8; 27:15; Ps. 97:7). Participation in the worship of other gods was forbidden (Exod. 23:24; 34:14, 17; Lev. 19:4; 20:4-5). Pagan idols were to be demolished (Exod. 23:24; 34:13; Deut. 7:5, 25; 12:1-3; Judg. 2:2; 6:28; 2 Kings 18:4; 23:14; 2 Chron. 31:1; 34:3-4). Covenants with pagans were forbidden for fear that worship of their idols might spread in Israel (Exod. 23:32; 34:12-15; Deut. 20:16-18). Although Israel did not always live up to the principles God revealed in His word, these were God's commandments.

Third, New Testament Christianity restates the Old Testament teaching that idolatry is sinful (Acts 15:20, 29; 17:16; 21:25; 1 Cor. 6:9; 8:4; 10:7, 14; 12:2; 2 Cor. 6:14-18; Gal. 5:20; 1 Thess. 1:9; 1 John 5:21; Rev. 21:8; 22:15). One who is involved in idolatry sins against God and cannot inherit the kingdom of heaven (Gal. 5:19-21).

Fourth, first century Christians were exclusive. The New Testament teaches that there is only one way to eternal salvation – through faith in Jesus. Jesus said it plainly:

Therefore I said to you that you will die in your sins; for if you do not believe that I am He, you will die in your sins (John 8:24).

Jesus said to him, "I am the way, the truth, and the life. No one comes to the Father except through Me" (John 14:6).

Peter preached the same truth before the Jewish Sanhedrin saying, "Let it be known to you all, and to all the people of Israel, that by the name of Jesus Christ of Nazareth, whom you crucified, whom God raised from the dead, by Him this man stands here before you whole. This is the 'stone which was rejected by you builders, which has become the chief cornerstone.' Nor is there salvation in any other, for there is no other name under heaven given among men by which we must be saved" (Acts 4:10-12).

The Great Commission said that salvation is only available through faith in Jesus saying, "Go into all the world and preach the gospel to every creature. He who believes and is baptized will be saved; but he who does not believe will be condemned" (Mark 16:15-16). Belief in Jesus is essential to salvation (John 3:16).

In commenting on the exclusivism of the gospel, D. A. Carson wrote,

This position teaches that the central claims of biblically faithful Christianity are true. Correspondingly, where the teachings of other religions conflict with these claims, they must necessarily be false. This stance brings with it certain views of who Jesus is, what the Bible is, and how salvation is achieved. Normally it is also held that salvation cannot be attained through the structures or claims of other religions. It does not hold that every other religion is wrong in every respect. Nor does it claim that all who claim to be Christians are saved, or right in every respect. It does insist that where other religions are contradicted by the gracious self-disclosure of Christ, they must necessarily be wrong. Until the modern period, this was virtually the unanimous view of Christians.[9]

Fifth, the early church believed in "one God," "one Lord," "one faith," and "one body" (Eph. 4:4-5). God would not tolerate even two religious bodies: one for Jews and one for Gentile

_____

[9] D. A. Carson, *The Gagging of God*, 27.

Christians; reconciliation to God occurs in only one body by the cross (Eph. 2:16).

Although Christianity was born in a pluralistic society, it was exclusive in its teaching about truth. If first century Christians took this stance toward all other religions, why should twenty-first century Christians who claim to believe in the same God and follow the same Lord take any different stance?

Conclusion

The principles of philosophical pluralism are contrary to divine revelation. Like modern Christians, first century Christians believed a doctrine that was not "politically correct" and was "out of step" with the time in which they lived. They faced the choice of being conformed to the philosophies of their times or adhering to the gospel, but they could not do both. Nor can we!

Questions

1. What is empirical pluralism? _____

   _____

2. Is empirical pluralism wrong? _____

   _____

3. What is philosophical pluralism? _____

   _____

4. What is wrong with philosophical pluralism? _____

   _____

5. Why is it significant that 66% of Americans agree that there is no absolute truth? _____

   _____

6. How will the rejection of an absolute truth affect efforts to evangelize? _____

   _____

7. How does philosophical pluralism affect pulpit preaching, according to D. A. Carson? _____

   _____

   _____

   Do you agree with his assessment? _____

8. What was the Roman attitude toward the many different religions of that day? _____

   _____

NOTES

_____

_____

_____

_____

_____

_____

9. How does pluralism differ from the Ten Commandments? _____

_____

10. What is the Bible's key area of disagreement with pluralism? _____

_____

11. What does John 8:32 teach that conflicts with pluralism? _____

_____

12. What attitude toward worshiping "other gods" did God command Israel to have? Why should our
    attitude toward worshiping other gods be any different? _____

_____

13. What verses in the New Testament show what the Christian's attitude toward the worship of other
    gods and the use of idols should be in the Christian era? _____

_____

14. What does Jesus say in John 8:24; 14:6 that conflicts with pluralism? _____

_____

_____

15. How does Mark 16:16 disagree with pluralism? _____

_____

Tolerance

Daniel Taylor wrote about intolerance in the January 11, 1999 issue of *Christianity Today*:

> It is the only serious sin left. Even murder has its mitigating factors, but not this one. It is the pariah sin, the charge that makes you untouchable without need for further explanation. The sin is intolerance, and the greatest sinners in late twentieth-century America are evangelical Christians. America is sick of intolerant people, and it's not going to tolerate them anymore.[1]

The charge of intolerance is a powerful weapon in the twenty-first century culture wars. It is a fatal blow (whether or not the charge is true is sometimes immaterial; many who have been castigated as homophobic or labeled as racial bigots are not guilty). When someone preaches that homosexuality is sinful is he guilty of the sin of intolerance? Since intolerance is an important issue facing twenty-first century Christians, we need to understand what is happening in our culture and what the Bible teaches on the subject.

How Did We Get Here?

In the belief system of post-modernism, there are no absolute truths. Truth is relative to the individual – what is true for one person is not necessarily true for anyone else. In post-modernism thought, every person has to understand the relativity of truth so that he will approve of everyone's views of truth. Belief in absolute truth leads to the conclusion that those not believing that truth are wrong (sinful). Efforts to turn one from his mistaken belief to the acceptance of the truth is condemned as proselytizing. Ironically, the "gospel" of relativism is perhaps the most "evangelistic" (proselytizing) of any religious movement in the United States and the least tolerant of disagreeing views.[2] It is also inconsistent. What makes "intolerance" a violation of ethics, unless there is some universal norm that has been violated? However, a post-modernist belief system denies that there is any universal moral law. From the perspective of the post-modernist belief system, "intolerance" should be wrong for one person but not for another, just the same as secularists think about homosexuality, but that is not the case.

Consider what happens when some nationally known person makes a statement that explicitly or implicitly condemns homosexuality as a sin. Does the media demonstrate its tolerance of that person's belief or does it make every effort to destroy the reputation of the one who expresses his honestly held opinion? We can think of such people as Anita Bryant, Phil Robertson (of *Duck Dynasty*), Mel Gibson, Donald Trump, etc. (the

---

[1] *Christianity Today* 43:1 (January 11, 1999), 43.

[2] D. A. Carson, *The Gagging of God*, 33.

Before and After	
Is he intolerant?	
James speaks his conviction that having an abortion is tantamount to murder. The local TV station reports the incident as an example of intolerance.	
Before	**After**

list keeps growing) who have been publicly blasted for expressing their conservative views about homosexuality. Suddenly, those who affirm that there are no absolutes are absolutely sure that this person's belief (that homosexuality is sinful) is *wrong* – not in the relative sense that in someone's belief system it is wrong, but in the absolute sense! In the name of tolerance, post-modernists are unwilling to tolerate another expressing his belief that homosexuality is sinful. In point of fact, the homosexual community is one of the most intolerant groups in America; they show no tolerance of one expressing a different point of view – the belief that those who practice and defend homosexuality are guilty of sin.[3]

Tolerance

Is tolerance a virtue? That depends upon one's definition of "tolerance." *Merriam-Webster* defines the word to mean "sympathy or indulgence for beliefs or practices differing from or conflicting with one's own."[4] Toleration is a virtue under this older definition, when one allows a person who disagrees to present his view

forcefully and vocally. In that understanding, one party allowed the other to openly and forthrightly disagree and reply to the other's position. Both parties are in quest of an objective truth on a given subject, both respect the other's honest quest to find that truth, and both recognize the danger of human fallibility. But tolerance does not mean that today.

Tolerance has been redefined to mean *"acceptance of different views."*[5] Carson commented about the change in definition as follows:

> To accept that a different or opposing position exists and deserves the right to exist is one thing; to accept the position itself means that one is no longer opposing it. The new tolerance suggests that actually accepting another's position means believing that position to be true, or at least as true as your own.[6]

> Intolerance is no longer a refusal to allow contrary opinions to say their piece in public, but must be understood to be any questioning or contradicting the view that all opinions are equal in value, that all worldviews have equal worth, that all stances are equally valid.[7]

S. D. Gaede said virtually the same thing.

> With few exceptions, multiculturalism is not argued today on the basis of promoting justice but on the grounds of inclusiveness. And the fundamental assumption is that it is good to be tolerant of different ideas and different perspectives. In other words, undergirding current thought on multiculturalism is not some sense of what is ultimately just and true, but a very deep moral and ontological relativism. Thus the argument for multiculturalism typically runs like this: Because all cultural perspectives are

---

[3] The homosexual lobby groups are beginning to resemble the McCarthyists. Named after Sen. Joseph McCarthy of Wisconsin, who was concerned about the spread of Communism in America, McCarthyism eventually took on a broader meaning to describe the excesses of similar efforts by other groups. The term is used more generally to describe reckless, unsubstantiated accusations against another. Because of McCarthyists' excessive practices and attacks, some of their victims suffered loss of employment and/or destruction of their careers. In the same way, homosexual lobby groups attack prominent people who express the belief that homosexuality is a sin, trying to force companies to fire that person or cut off his endorsements, thus ending his public career, to the extent that they have the ability to do so.

[4] *http://www.merriam-webster.com/dictionary/tolerance.*

[5] D. A. Carson, *The Intolerance of Tolerance*, 3.

[6] *Ibid.*

[7] Carson, *op. cit.*, 12.

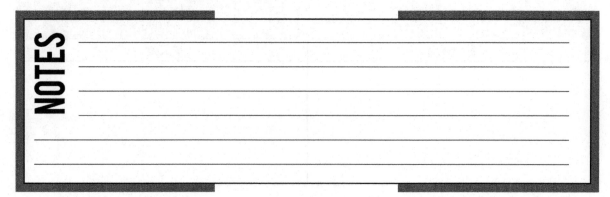

NOTES

_____
_____
_____
_____
_____
_____

equally valid, every idea or perspective ought to be included. Indeed, to be exclusive about truth (to assert that one can distinguish truth and error) is bad, while to be inclusive of all truth claims is good. The *raison d'etre* (i.e. "reason for existence") of multiculturalism becomes tolerance.[8]

On the one hand, the old view recognized that there is an objective truth that both parties are in a quest to find; both participants believe that the best way to obtain objective truth is to allow all parties freedom to search for that truth and present the evidence supporting one's position, giving interested hearers the evidence to decide which view (if either) is correct. On the other hand, the modern view argues that there is no absolute and exclusive truth, so all views should have equal standing. However, there is absolutely no tolerance for one who states his belief in absolute truth. In the post-modernist view, tolerance means recognizing that both views are equally true. *Ironically, the new definition of tolerance has led to the older intolerance!*

One must understand that: (1) tolerance presupposes that one objects to the thing he tolerates. One cannot be said to tolerate that which he accepts and approves. Modern liberalism is not tolerant; one cannot be said to tolerate homosexuality when he believes that it is right and has no objection to it. If you want to know if modern liberals are tolerant, ask them if they tolerate Rush Limbaugh, evangelical preachers who condemn homosexuality as a sin, neo-Nazi racists, etc. (2) Tolerance also requires withholding of power. If the reason one does not act is because he is powerless to do so, he is only impotent; if he has the power to act and does not act to coerce certain behavior, he is tolerant.

---

[8] S. D. Gaede, *When Tolerance Is No Virtue*, 37-38.

(3) Everyone is intolerant of some things (think about liberalism's list of what it cannot tolerate: racism, pro-life, homophobia, sexism, etc.). The liberal element of society does not tolerate those with whom they disagree. Rather, they make every effort to silence and squelch the voices of those who disagree (e.g., on homosexuality, creation, pro-life, etc.).

Is There an Absolute Truth?

Think about tolerance and the denial of absolute truth for a moment. Johnny is in the second grade when his teacher gives him a math test that includes the problem 2 + 2 = _____. Johnny answered 3, Suzie answered 5, and Patricia answered 4. In the modern view that there are no absolutes, all three answers are equally right. One answer is Johnny's view of truth, one is Suzie's view of truth, and one is Patricia's view of truth. Following modern tolerance theory, the teacher would be narrow-minded, dogmatic, and intolerant should she pronounce that Johnny and Suzie are wrong and Patricia is right. The post-modernist view of truth does not work very well in mathematics! So we go to English class where a test is also being given. This question addresses subject/verb agreement. The question asks one to select the correct verb for the subject of this sentence: "Johnny and Suzie (*is/are*) in the fourth grade." Should Johnny answer "is" and Suzie answer "are," then both are right, if there are no absolute truths. Though the position of no absolutes seems ridiculous in math and English, that there are no absolutes is what one must believe when the issue shifts from mathematics to religion and morals.

However, according to Biblical teaching, there is an absolute truth, not based on the superior intellect or privileged position of one person

---

NOTES

_____

_____

_____

_____

_____

_____

_____

versus the other, but because the Omniscient God has revealed His objective truth to all of mankind. Jesus said about God's word, "thy word is truth" (John 17:17; cf. 2 Sam. 7:28; Ps. 119:142, 151). Because God has spoken, man can know and obey the truth (John 8:32).

Although the post-modern definition of tolerance denies that there is any absolute truth, those who hold to this definition can never consistently apply it.[9] The very statement of the belief leads to this self-contradiction: "It is absolutely true that there are no absolute truths!" Furthermore, post-modernists believe that a woman absolutely does have the right to choose to have an abortion, that homosexuals should be given the same rights to marriage as heterosexuals, and other similar inflexible beliefs. For a Christian to accept the post-modernist/ humanist/naturalist doctrine of relative truth leads to a rejection of the teachings of the Bible.

The Bible and Tolerance

Post-modernism grounds its view of "tolerance" on the denial of an absolute truth – one should accept that another's belief system/ morality is equally as valid as his own – because there is no absolute right and wrong. However, the Bible's teaching about tolerance rests on different principles. They are:

A person's faith and obedience must be voluntary to be acceptable to God. If one were to take a gun and force a person to be baptized, that baptism would not meet the demands of

---

[9] S. D. Gaede wrote, "If you are intolerant of someone who is intolerant, then you have necessarily violated your own principle. But if you tolerate those who are intolerant, you keep your principle but sacrifice your responsibility to your principle" (*When Tolerance Is No Virtue*, 23).

the gospel. Bible baptism requires that it be preceded by faith and repentance. The will of man voluntarily believes in and submits to the Lord Jesus Christ. Free-will obedience is taught in Scripture (Josh. 24:15). Even God tolerates sinners acting with high-handed rebellion against His will; He does not force sinners to obey Him.

Christ commanded that one love his neighbor as himself (Matt. 22:39) and treat him as he wishes to be treated (Matt. 7:12 – "Do unto others as you would have them do unto you"). Biblical tolerance is grounded in brotherly love.

Though God tolerates all forms of conduct, He does not approve all forms of conduct. For example, God does not accept all acts of worship (see Cain and Abel, Gen. 4; Nadab and Abihu, Lev. 10:1-2; the worship of Israel at Bethel and Dan, 1 Kings 12:25-33). God defines as sinful certain kinds of behavior (see the Ten Commandments: "thou shalt not" ... kill, commit adultery, steal, bear false witness, covet). Though God does not force obedience, He does not approve of disobedience. He tolerates this sinful conduct inasmuch as He does not immediately punish it, but He does not approve it.

The Biblical teaching on tolerance is not simple. Tolerance involves an individual's relationships with other individuals, the government (which can be broken down into several categories), and the church. Let's consider each of these:

1. Individual relationships. We Christians cannot escape the environment of the world in which we live; we have association and contacts with non-Christians who are covetous, extortioners, idolaters, etc., that cannot be avoided because we live in the world (1 Cor. 5:10). While not approving of the conduct of such sinners, we have the obligation to "love

NOTES

_____
_____
_____
_____
_____
_____
_____

our neighbor as ourselves" (Lev. 19:18; Matt. 22:39; Gal. 5:14; Jas. 2:8). In the Parable of the Good Samaritan, Jesus taught His disciples to be a neighbor to one's fellowman who is in need (Luke 10:25-37). Daniel lived in a society that worshiped other gods than he did and that bowed before images. In that society, Daniel worked alongside of Chaldean "wise men," including astrologers, magicians, and soothsayers (Dan. 2:12, 18, 27). After interpreting Nebuchadnezzar's dream, Daniel was made chief over these men (Dan. 2:48). He worked with these men in spite of their significant religious differences. Likewise, Nehemiah worked as cupbearer to a Persian king, although he had different religious convictions than the Persians. Mordecai worked with Haman and tolerated him in spite of his despicable efforts to destroy God's people (Esther).

Tolerance in the old definition is easily understood. Christians do not force obedience on anyone; we invite all of mankind to join us in open discussion of God's word that we might "search the Scriptures daily to find out whether these things are so" (Acts 17:11). We, therefore, defend the right of others to present their understanding of an objective truth that we also are seeking to find. However, tolerance in the new definition (all beliefs are equally valid) is contrary to divine revelation. A Christian cannot give approval to any viewpoint that is contrary to the revealed word of God, whether that be in areas of doctrine, church organization, or morality. One view of truth is not equal to all other views (e.g., "murder is righteous" does not have the same moral validity as "thou shalt not kill," nor does "Jesus is the illegitimate son of Palestinian peasants" have the same truth value as "Jesus is the Son of God").

2. Government relationships. We must be careful in working through tolerance issues to distinguish between personal tolerance and what governments choose to enforce as their civil law. There is no government that is tolerant of every point of view and conduct. Every society has its own laws which are enforced with punishments ranging from fines, to incarceration, to capital punishment. No government is tolerant of extortion, stealing, kidnapping, rape, treason, murder, etc. It is ridiculous to speak as if toleration means that all forms of conduct are equally right, that all value judgments are equal, autonomous, and relative. What rapist would try to defend himself in either the judicial courts or the court of public opinion based on such reasoning?

What does the Bible teach about governments and tolerance? The Bible gives no detailed information about ancient governments; we learn bits and pieces of information that are recorded in an incidental way. The Torah (Gen. – Deut.) contains God's law for both the individual and the nation of Israel. During its independent national existence, Israel enforced its own national laws, some of which were revealed by God and some of which laws were established by men as they regulated government in their country. When God revealed His will to mankind, that revelation included individual requirements and national/government regulations. Ideally, Israel was a theocracy; realistically, Israel was frequently in rebellion to God's law and, in creating their own laws, included many things that were an abomination to God. Like all governments, Israel had legislation that proscribed certain forms of conduct: murder (Exod. 20:13), stealing (Exod. 20:15), incest (Lev. 18:6-20), bestiality (Lev. 18:23), kidnapping (Deut. 24:7), etc. Israelite punishments for various crimes ranged from

NOTES

_____
_____
_____
_____
_____
_____

beatings (Deut. 25:3) to capital punishment (Exod. 21:12-14).

The New Testament leaves the responsibility of proscribing what is illegitimate behavior that is punishable by governments to uninspired men. God did not write a constitution and legal codes for all governments as He did for Israel. Though He has ordained government (Rom. 13:1ff.), He left it to uninspired men to develop their own legal codes, based on principles of righteousness and justice. No government is perfect, so Americans should not expect their own government to so be. Sometimes government makes terrible laws (such as the Dred Scot decision which declared that Blacks are "beings of an inferior order, and altogether unfit to associate with the white race, either in social or political relations, and so far inferior that they had no rights which the white man was bound to respect").[10] We can look at several modern decisions that are no better (e.g., *Roe v. Wade* which implies the non-personhood of the fetus in the womb in order to make abortion a woman's right to choose). Governments are fallible, human efforts designed to run a civil state.

Christians Living under Governments

The civil government under which Christianity was established, whether one looks at the Judean province or the Roman Empire, was not tolerant of dissent. The Apostles had their lives threatened (Acts 5:33) and were beaten by the Jewish officials for preaching the gospel (Acts 5:40). Herod Agrippa I put James, the brother of John, to death (Acts 12:1-2) and intended also to put Peter to death for the "crime" of preaching Christ (Acts 12:3-19). The Roman government executed Paul (2 Tim. 4:6-8), Antipas (Rev. 2:13), and many others. In the book of Revelation, the Roman government is pictured as an ally of false religion, intent on destroying the people of God (Rev. 12-19).

Most of what the Bible teaches about Christians living under governments describes living under repressive and intolerant governments – governments that sometimes put to death a person because of his faith in God. The Bible teaches Christians how to survive during such intolerable circumstances.

Conclusion

True tolerance describes conduct that one has toward those with whom he disagrees; even if a truly tolerant person had the power to stop them from teaching what they believe, he would not. Tolerance is necessary because we recognize our own human fallibility. We are on a quest to learn objective truth. We think we have found it, but we invite those with whom we disagree to reply to our preaching and engage us in discussion and debate in our common quest for the saving truth revealed in God's word.

---

[10] *http://en.wikipedia.org/wiki/Dred_Scott_v._Sandford.*

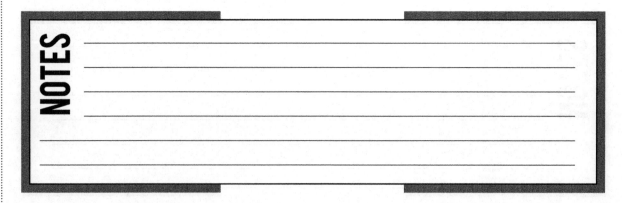

Questions

1. Give an example of someone who lost his job or was publicly attacked for opposing homo-sexuality. _____

2. Why is "tolerance" such a hot issue in modern society?_____
   _____

3. Why is it inconsistent for homosexuals to charge others with being intolerant?_____
   _____

4. How are homosexual groups similar to McCarthyists?_____
   _____

5. Define tolerance:
   a. Old definition: _____
   b. New definition: _____

6. On what grounds do the following believe in "tolerance"?
   a. Post-modernists:_____
   b. Christians:_____

7. What three conditions are essential for one to be "tolerant" of another's position?
   a. _____
   b. _____
   c. _____

8. What are some things modern society has absolutely no tolerance for? _____
   _____

9. What is meant by "relativism"? _____
   _____

10. How does one know what is truth (John 17:17)?_____
    _____

11. How can one know that he is able to understand that truth (John 8:32)? _____
    _____

NOTES
_____
_____
_____
_____
_____
_____

12. Why can one not consistently be tolerant of all beliefs? _____

_____

13. Give a Bible example that shows tolerance toward individuals with whom one disagrees? _____

_____

14. Give some examples of behavior that our nation will not tolerate. _____

_____

15. Is American intolerance of a given behavior different from Israel's civil laws that regulated sinful conduct? _____

_____

16. Cite examples of American civil laws that are completely misguided. _____

_____

NOTES
_____
_____
_____
_____
_____
_____

The Bible and Tolerance

In this lesson, we want to look at what the Bible teaches about tolerance in both definitions of the term. Does the Bible teach that religions that teach doctrines different from the Bible should be free to propagate their views? Does the Bible teach that all religious beliefs stand on equal footing, that there is no one right way to the exclusion of all others?

The study will be divided into two parts: (a) God's teaching under the Old Testament, when Israel was governed by national laws; (b) God's teaching under the New Testament when God's people are not a political state.

Israel's Religious Laws

When God gave Israel commandments about the organization of its state, the "separation of church and state" was no part of Israel's constitution. Religion and state were interwoven, similar to the manner in which it is interwoven in modern Islamic states. The Ten Commandments was the constitutional document of Israelite society and its laws included the following laws related to worship:

I am the LORD your God, who brought you out of the land of Egypt, out of the house of bondage. You shall have no other gods before Me.

You shall not make for yourself a carved image, or any likeness of anything that is in heaven above, or that is in the earth beneath, or that is in the water under the earth; you shall not bow down to them nor serve them. For I, the LORD your God, am a jealous God, visiting the iniquity of the fathers on the children to the third and fourth generations of those who hate Me, but showing mercy to thousands, to those who love Me and keep My commandments.

You shall not take the name of the LORD your God in vain, for the LORD will not hold him guiltless who takes His name in vain.

Remember the Sabbath day, to keep it holy (Exod. 20:2-8).

God commanded that worship of other gods should not be tolerated in Israel.

You shall have no other gods before Me. You shall not make for yourself a carved image – any likeness of anything that is in heaven above, or that is in the earth beneath, or that is in the water under the earth; you shall not bow down to them nor serve them. For I, the LORD your God, am a jealous God, visiting the iniquity of the fathers upon the children to the third and fourth generations of those who hate Me (Deut. 5:7-9).

God announced beforehand that, if Israel started serving other gods, they would perish from off the land He gave to them (Deut. 4:23-27; 6:14-15; 8:19-20; 11:26-28; 30:17-18).

Before and After	
How would you react to this suggestion?	
One should study the Old Testament to learn Israel's laws in order to apply them in America.	
Before	**After**

Participation in the worship of other gods was not only forbidden; Israel was commanded to eradicate false religions out of their land.

> You shall not bow down to their gods, nor serve them, nor do according to their works; but you shall utterly overthrow them and completely break down their sacred pillars (Exod. 23:24).

> But you shall destroy their altars, break their sacred pillars, and cut down their wooden images (for you shall worship no other god, for the LORD, whose name is Jealous, is a jealous God) (Exod. 34:13-14).

> ... then you shall drive out all the inhabitants of the land from before you, destroy all their engraved stones, destroy all their molded images, and demolish all their high places (Num. 33:52).

> But thus you shall deal with them: you shall destroy their altars, and break down their sacred pillars, and cut down their wooden images, and burn their carved images with fire (Deut. 7:5).

> You shall burn the carved images of their gods with fire; you shall not covet the silver or gold that is on them, nor take it for yourselves, lest you be snared by it; for it is an abomination to the LORD your God (Deut. 7:25).

> And you shall destroy their altars, break their sacred pillars, and burn their wooden images with fire; you shall cut down the carved images of their gods and destroy their names from that place (Deut. 12:3).

It was not God's will that the modern "live and let live" attitude toward different religions exist in the ancient state of Israel.

Whereas modern practice is to allow any false doctrine to be taught in a society, with the only response being that others have the equal right to reply to his teachings, in ancient Israel, the false prophet was to be put to death.

> If there arises among you a prophet or a dreamer of dreams, and he gives you a sign or a wonder, and the sign or the wonder comes to pass, of which he spoke to you, saying, "Let us go after other gods" – which you have not known – "and let us serve them": you shall not listen to the words of that prophet or that dreamer of dreams, for the LORD your God is testing you to know whether you love the LORD your God with all your heart and with all your soul. You shall walk after the LORD your God and fear Him, and keep His commandments and obey His voice, and you shall serve Him and hold fast to Him. But that prophet or that dreamer of dreams shall be put to death, because he has spoken in order to turn you away from the LORD your God, who brought you out of the land of Egypt and redeemed you from the house of bondage, to entice you from the way in which the LORD your God commanded you to walk. So you shall put away the evil from your midst (Deut. 13:1-5; cf. 18:20-22).

An example of the application of this law is the contest on Mt. Carmel in the days of King Ahab. Jezebel had strengthened Baalism in the northern kingdom of Israel. God caused a famine to occur in the land to show divine displeasure. After three and one-half years, God sent Elijah to Mt. Carmel where a contest was held between the prophets of Baal and Elijah. Elijah said, "How long will you falter between two opinions? If the LORD is God, follow Him; but if Baal, follow him" (1 Kings 18:21). The contest was for both the prophets of Baal and Elijah, the prophet of Yahweh, to prepare an altar to sacrifice to their respective God; the God who lit the fire on the altar would be the God whom Israel would serve. The prophets of Baal failed, but God lit the fire on Elijah's altar. On that day, 450 prophets of Baal were put to death (1 Kings 18).

Not only were false prophets not tolerated in Israelite society, the one who secretly worshiped

NOTES
_____
_____
_____
_____
_____

other gods was to be exposed, even by his near relatives.

> If your brother, the son of your mother, your son or your daughter, the wife of your bosom, or your friend who is as your own soul, secretly entices you, saying, "Let us go and serve other gods," which you have not known, neither you nor your fathers, of the gods of the people which are all around you, near to you or far off from you, from one end of the earth to the other end of the earth, you shall not consent to him or listen to him, nor shall your eye pity him, nor shall you spare him or conceal him; but you shall surely kill him; your hand shall be first against him to put him to death, and afterward the hand of all the people. And you shall stone him with stones until he dies, because he sought to entice you away from the LORD your God, who brought you out of the land of Egypt, from the house of bondage. So all Israel shall hear and fear, and not again do such wickedness as this among you (Deut. 13:6-11; cf. 17:1-7).

Should one of the towns in Israel depart from the Lord to follow another god, the civil responsibility of the nation was to destroy that town.

> If you hear someone in one of your cities, which the LORD your God gives you to dwell in, saying, "Corrupt men have gone out from among you and enticed the inhabitants of their city, saying, 'Let us go and serve other gods'" – which you have not known – then you shall inquire, search out, and ask diligently. And if it is indeed true and certain that such an abomination was committed among you, you shall surely strike the inhabitants of that city with the edge of the sword – utterly destroying it, all that is in it and its livestock, with the edge of the sword. And you shall gather all its plunder into the middle of the street, and completely burn with fire the city and all its plunder, for the LORD your God. It shall be a heap forever; it shall not be built again. So none of the accursed things shall remain in your hand, that the LORD may turn from the fierceness of His anger and show you mercy, have compassion on you and multiply you, just as He swore to your fathers, because you have listened to the voice of the LORD your God, to keep all His commandments which I command you today, to do what is right in the eyes of the LORD your God (Deut. 13:12-18).

An incident happened shortly after the conquest under Joshua in which the tribes that were located on the eastern side of the Jordan erected an altar resembling the one at the Tabernacle. The tribes west of the Jordan thought that this was being built as an alternative worship site and prepared themselves to punish the apostate tribes. Upon investigation they found that this was not the purpose of building the altar and withdrew their threat against them (Josh. 22:10-34). The incident shows how the law of Deuteronomy 13:12-18 was to be enforced in Israel.

The obligation of the combined tribes to enforce discipline on a wayward city was recognized not only with reference to its central place of worship but also in areas of morality. In the period of the Judges, an Ephraimite man was returning from visiting his father-in-law in Bethlehem-Judah (see Judg. 19). On his way home, he stopped for the night in Gibeah of the tribe of Benjamin. There a gang of men raped his wife. When they were finished abusing her, she crawled to the door of the home where her husband was and passed out. The next morning, he took his wife home. The husband cut his wife into twelve pieces and sent a portion to each of the twelve tribes and said, "No such deed has been done or seen from the day that the children of Israel came up from the land of Egypt until this day. Consider it, confer, and speak up!" (Judg. 19:30). The nation organized against Gibeah,

NOTES

_____
_____
_____
_____
_____
_____

but the Benjamites came to their defense. A civil war ensued that almost exterminated the tribe of Benjamin (Judg. 20).

One must conclude that ancient Israel was not a tolerant society in either the older definition or the twenty-first century meaning of the term.[1] Why was this the case? The answer lies in the fact that Israel was a theocracy. "Theocracy" is a form of government in which a deity is officially recognized as the civil Ruler and official policy is governed by officials regarded as divinely guided, or is pursuant to the doctrine of a particular religion or religious group.[2] In a theocracy, where God is considered the king on the throne, one who rebels against God is guilty of treason. Article Three of the United States Constitution says,

> Treason against the United States, shall consist only in levying War against them, or in adhering to their Enemies, giving them Aid and Comfort. No Person shall be convicted of Treason unless on the Testimony of two Witnesses to the same overt Act, or on Confession in open Court.

> The Congress shall have Power to declare the Punishment of Treason, but no Attainder of Treason shall work Corruption of Blood, or Forfeiture except during the Life of the Person attainted.[3]

---

[1] There were times when Israel, in disobedience to God, tolerated idolatry and participated in pagan worship. But God's will was not to allow these practices in the nation of Israel.

[2] http://en.wikipedia.org/wiki/Theocracy. Merriam-Webster's definition is "a form of government in which a country is ruled by religious leaders....government in a state by immediate divine guidance or by officials who are regarded as divinely inspired" (http://www.merriam-webster.com/dictionary/theocracy), accessed 4/9/2014.

[3] http://en.wikipedia.org/wiki/Article_Three_of_the_United_States_Constitution, accessed 4/9/2014.

In the United States, the punishment for treason is "death, or shall be imprisoned not less than five years and fined under this title but not less than $10,000; and shall be incapable of holding any office under the United States."[4] One must interpret Israel's law about apostasy in worshiping another God in the context of Israel being a theocracy, where rejection of Yahweh to follow Baal was tantamount to refusing to be subject to one person as king and claiming allegiance to a rival king. The United States faced a similar situation to Israel during the Civil War (1861-1865) when part of the country gave allegiance to Abraham Lincoln and part to Jefferson Davis. Cities and states that aligned themselves with Davis were attacked in the same way as Israel attacked the Benjamites who supported Gibeah (Judg. 19). To interpret these Old Testament passages outside a non-theocratic context treats unfairly its teaching.

In the New Testament

As one approaches the New Testament, he recognizes that, in Christ, God is not dealing with a nation, but with Christians and a church. Jesus said, "My kingdom is not of this world. If My kingdom were of this world, My servants would fight, so that I should not be delivered to the Jews; but now My kingdom is not from here" (John 18:36). In the New Testament, the church sometimes exists in a hostile environment; rarely were God's people the majority in a sympathetic society. Throughout history, the church is more likely to be displayed as the victim of intolerance than the perpetrator of intolerance.[5]

---

[4] http://en.wikipedia.org/wiki/Treason#United_States, accessed 4/9/2014.

[5] There have been times when church and state have been so intertwined that the arm of the state was used to enforce religious persecution against dissenters

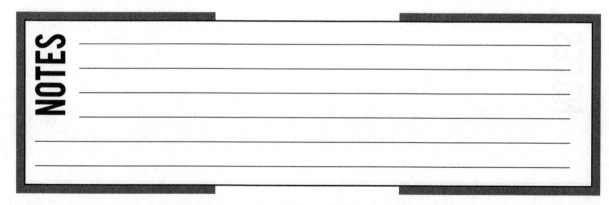
NOTES

Neither Jesus nor the early church was tolerated by the Jewish leadership of the first century. The gospels record numerous conflicts between Jesus and the Jewish leaders (see for example, conflict narratives in the Gospels: Mark 2:1-12, 13-28; 3:1-6; Matt. 9:34; 12:1-15, 22-37; 15:1-20; etc.). Jesus's disciples were not tolerated by the Jewish hierarchy. There is evidence of exclusion from the synagogue of those who followed Jesus, although it is difficult to determine whether these were isolated or widespread instances (Luke 6:22; John 9:22, 34; 12:42; 16:2; 19:38). The crucifixion of Jesus caused His disciples to be afraid for their lives (John 20:19). In the book of Acts, Jewish intolerance toward the leaders of the church took different forms: (a) Reproaches (Acts 22:22, 23; 2 Cor. 6:8; Heb. 10:33); (b) Bitter Hatred (Acts 9:1; 26:11); (c) Efforts to silence the Word (Acts 4:5-18; 5:27-40; 1 Thess. 2:16) (d) Conspiracy (John 12:10; Acts 5:33; 14:2; 17:5-13; 23:12-22; 26:21); (e) Imprisonment (Acts 4:3; 5:18; 8:3; 9:2, 14; 12:3-4; Heb. 10:34); (f) Banishment (Acts 8:1; 13:50); (g) Corporal Punishment (Mark 13:9; Acts 22:19, 24; 2 Cor. 11:23-25); (h) Death (Acts 7:57, 58; 12:1-2; 22:4, 5; 26:10). If Jewish leaders believed Jesus was a false prophet, their actions may be defended as obedience to the law forbidding false prophets in their midst; however, outsiders viewed their conduct as motivated by politics (Matt. 27:18; Mark 15:10). Jewish religious leaders brought political pressure against Pilate to persuade him to hand Jesus over for crucifixion (John 19:12).

One never reads of the church using either corporal or capital punishment against those who taught another gospel or apostatized from the faith.[6] When the church and state become intertwined so that the state enforces church discipline, both church and state are acting contrary to what God authorized either to do. In regard to the church not using corporeal or capital punishment of those who violated its teachings, a break with synagogue practices is noted.[7]

The church did not tolerate within its fellowship those who taught another gospel/doctrine or those who lived immoral lives. The church was commanded to withdraw itself from the Corinthian fornicator (1 Cor. 5; cf. Matt. 18:15-17), those who walk disorderly (2 Thess. 3:6, 14), and those who cause divisions and offences contrary to the doctrine they had been taught by the apostles (Rom. 16:17-18; 2 John 9-11). Even in the case of exclusion/withdrawal of fellowship, the erring disciple is to be treated not as an enemy, but exhorted as a brother (2 Thess. 3:14). The book of Revelation speaks of two churches that were condemned for tolerating false teachers in their midst:

> *Pergamus:* But I have a few things against you, because you have there those who hold the doctrine of Balaam, who taught Balak to put a stumbling block before the children of Israel,

---

to the faith. While one admits that the church-state persecution was wrong, he also must recognize that the "church" side of the church-state institution was not the Lord's church. Instead, it was a religio-political organization.

---

[6] The case of Ananias and Sapphira was not the church using capital punishment, as would be the case if they were taken outside of the building and stoned, but of God's immediate miraculous judgment against the sinners (Acts 5:1-11).

[7] The synagogue used both corporeal and capital punishment against those who taught something they disapproved. People were expelled from the synagogues (Luke 6:22; John 9:22, 34), beaten with stripes (2 Cor. 11:24), and stoned (2 Cor. 11:25; Acts 14:19).

NOTES

_____
_____
_____
_____
_____
_____

to eat things sacrificed to idols, and to commit sexual immorality (Rev. 2:14).

Thyatira: Nevertheless I have a few things against you, because you allow that woman Jezebel, who calls herself a prophetess, to teach and seduce My servants to commit sexual immorality and eat things sacrificed to idols (Rev. 2:20).

The instructions regarding fellowship must not be understood in the context of a political institution (such as government), but more in the context of a social institution setting its boundaries, albeit in this case under divine guidance. Every social group determines its boundaries for membership. Honor societies in schools determine who is included/ excluded based on grade point averages; work associations define who can/cannot be a member. Likewise, the church is a type of social association whose boundaries for inclusion in the group have been set under divine guidance. These boundaries include: (a) One has to be a Christian (to hear and believe the gospel, repent of his sins, confess his faith in Christ, and be baptized in water); (b) One has to maintain faithfulness to the gospel. Those who do not do these things are excluded. In defining its boundaries, the church is no more intolerant than is any other social group within a society (such as occurs when the National Honor Society expels a member whose grade point average has fallen below minimum standards).

Coercion

The Bible does not teach that one should coerce another to obey the gospel. By contrast, Muslim societies believe in coercion. D. A. Carson wrote,

Where Muslims are in control, Muslim thought about non-Muslims in the society is quite clear.

The choices are three: kill them (under certain circumstances), convert them, or *dhimmitude.* The *dhimmis* (i.e., the non-Muslims in the culture) are inevitably placed in an inferior position. They may pay more taxes; they may not attempt to convert Muslims to their own faith; any compromise they propose to stabilize their position will inevitably be taken as a mark of their inferiority and weakness, for, from a devout Muslim perspective, the *dhimmis* frankly owe homage to Allah and his people.[8]

In some respects, the secular attitude toward religious people resembles that of the Muslims' view of the *dhimmis.* Carson adds, "... the secularist wants all other religions to retreat into the private sphere, he or she insists that secularists have the right to control the public sphere because they are right – completely unaware that they are trying to impose their worldview on others who disagree with it."[9]

Conclusion

From this survey, one immediately sees that the Bible is not a pluralist document that views all truth claims as equally valid and, therefore, does not approve different religious beliefs and moral practices. The Bible is a divine revelation from God – objective truth – that must be believed and obeyed. American pluralism, with its belief that all value judgments are equally valid, is not a virtue. The commitment to the belief that there is an objective truth and the recognition of our human fallibility is what makes us committed to giving everyone the right to be heard, to defend his belief with whatever evidence he can present. S. D. Gaede described the relationship between truth and tolerance as follows:

First, it must be assumed that truth exists and that it is worth preserving and passing on to

---

[8] D. A. Carson, *The Intolerance of Tolerance,* 119-120.

[9] *Ibid.,* 121.

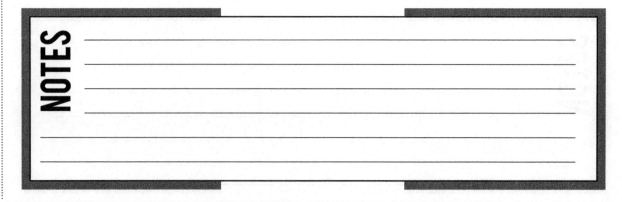

NOTES

future generations. And second, tolerance needs to be understood not as an end but as a means, a crucial ingredient in the preservation and cultivation of truth. Under such assumptions tolerance is not something we celebrate but something that we acknowledge as a necessity in a fallen world. What we celebrate, instead, is the truth. It is the truth we honor, it is the truth we cherish, and it is truth on which we stake our lives.[10]

Toleration for others' beliefs because we recognize human fallibility is the tolerance which the Bible teaches. Withholding the truth from someone for fear that you might offend him is not loving or kind (for example, not to express disagreement with someone who believes in the flat earth theory). A doctor who knows that one has a severe, but treatable, heart disease, but does not tell his patient of his condition because it might hurt his feelings, is a worthless physician. Even though a segment of society might accuse one of being intolerant, Christians have the moral obligation to teach others the gospel.

---

[10] S. D. Gaede, *When Tolerance Is No Virtue*, 109.

Questions

1. How were religion and government intertwined under Israel's theocracy?_____

   _____

2. How do the Ten Commandments show that all religious beliefs and practices are not equally valid? _____

   _____

3. Why was Israel intolerant of pagan religions (Exod. 23:24; 34:13-14; etc.)? _____

   _____

4. Why did God demand that false prophets be put to death (Deut. 13:1-5; 18:20-22)? _____

   _____

5. How were Israelite worshipers of pagan gods treated (Deut. 13:1-56; 17:1-7)?_____

   _____

6. What was to be done to an apostate city (Deut. 13:12-18)?_____

   _____

7. How does Israel being a theocracy affect her intolerance of worshiping another god? _____

   _____

8. What evidence is there for the church using corporeal punishment to enforce church law? _____

   _____

NOTES

_____

_____

_____

_____

_____

_____

9. Contrast what should be done with an apostate under the Old and New Testament laws. _____

_____

10. Why did the early church not tolerate unrighteous people within its fellowship (1 Cor. 5:1-11)?___

_____

11. Name some other organizations that discipline their members. _____

_____

12. What difference exists between the Bible and Koran with reference to using coercion to compel citizens to comply with its teaching?_____

_____

13. How are secularists and Muslims alike in reference to tolerance? _____

_____

NOTES

_____

_____

_____

_____

_____

In the Absence of Truth

Previously, we have shown that post-modernism inconsistently and absolutely teaches that there are no absolute truths. What happens in a culture in which there are no absolute truths? This question is particularly relevant as the American culture is becoming more secular and the Christian value system is more widely rejected.

What Is Truth?

When Jesus stood on trial before Pilate, Jesus said, "My kingdom is not of this world. If My kingdom were of this world, My servants would fight, so that I should not be delivered to the Jews; but now My kingdom is not from here." Pilate zeroed in on Jesus's reference to "His kingdom." He said to Jesus, "Are You a king then?" Jesus answered, "You say rightly that I am a king. For this cause I was born, and for this cause I have come into the world, that I should bear witness to the truth. Everyone who is of the truth hears My voice." Pilate said to Him, "What is truth?" (John 18:36-38). Pilate's flippant response pinpoints the issue for those who reject God's word as absolute truth. If not God's word, what then is truth?

S. D. Gaeda commented on how man has become his own god. He wrote:

> We choose beliefs the way we choose an entrée at a restaurant, taking whatever juicy morsel pleases our palates. This not only puts the self at the center of choice-making activity – thereby erecting a new overarching worldview, with the self playing god – but also puts great pressure on those who are trying to persuade others to adopt their beliefs.
>
> . . .
>
> Having pretty much decided that truth is not attainable, we have made tolerance of a plurality of truths a virtue. Having no truths worth defending, we have made nondefensiveness a mark of distinction.
>
> G.K. Chesterton once observed that "tolerance is the virtue of the man without convictions," and that seems to describe modern men and women fairly accurately.[1]

When one rejects the Biblical value system, with what shall he replace it? And when that newly accepted value system is breached, what coercion should be used to enforce that value system? If there is no right, there is no wrong.[2]

_____

[1] S. D. Gaede, *When Tolerance Is No Virtue*, 27-28.

[2] Significantly, pluralism leads to the conclusion that there is no orthodoxy or heterodoxy. Who do you know

Before and After	
How do you react to this?	
A group of abortion protestors are gathered at the Planned Parenthood clinic. The TV news reports the event describing these protestors as a group of religious bigots or zealots who are trying to impose their moral values on others	
Before	**After**

The fact of the matter is that "evil" is a word that can hardly be used today. On March 8, 1983, President Ronald Reagan gave what has been dubbed his "Evil Empire Speech," in which he said,

> During my first press conference as president, in answer to a direct question, I pointed out that, as good Marxist-Leninists, the Soviet leaders have openly and publicly declared that the only morality they recognize is that which will further their cause, which is world revolution. I think I should point out I was only quoting Lenin, their guiding spirit, who said in 1920 that they repudiate all morality that proceeds from supernatural ideas – that's their name for religion – or ideas that are outside class conceptions. Morality is entirely subordinate to the interests of class war. And everything is moral that is necessary for the annihilation of the old exploiting social order and for uniting the proletariat.[3]

Being under control of the liberalism, the media's response was uniformly negative to Reagan's speech. One blogger summarized the reaction saying, "Reagan was called every name in the book – dangerous, simplistic, outrageous, crazy. He was compared to the Ayatollah Khomeini and was said to have a 'holy war mentality.' And those were the polite responses. The charge of 'red-baiting' was leveled by House Speaker Tip O'Neill, and *Newsweek* reported that Reagan was reverting to his old ways as a 'cold warrior.'"[4] Though unpopular among the elite,

Reagan's speech identified a serious problem for the position of those who reject Christian values: How does one determine what is right and wrong? For those who reject the Supernatural, morality is determined by man, whether the most powerful men or the largest majority of men in a given society.

Writing about the Killing Fields of Cambodia,[5] David Aikman said,

> In the West today, there is a pervasive consent to the notion of moral relativism, a reluctance to admit that absolute evil can and does exist. This makes it especially difficult for some to accept the fact that the Cambodian experience is something far worse than a revolutionary aberration. Rather, it is the deadly logical consequence of an atheistic, man-centered system of values, enforced by fallible human beings with total power, who believe, with Marx, that morality is whatever the powerful define it to be and, with Mao, that power grows from gun barrels.[6]

After the attack on the Twin Towers on 9/11/01, America tried to grasp the evil that had happened. There was a brief flurry of discussion about evil, but this quickly passed. Edward Rothstein quoted Richard J. Bernstein, a philosopher at the New School University as follows: "It is almost as if

---

among denominational preachers who is a heretic by today's standards? Since "there are no absolute truths" is the only absolute truth in the secularist creed, those who claim that there is absolute truth are the only heretics. Ironically, the result is that Bible believers are the heretics, according to pluralism.

[3] *http://voicesofdemocracy.umd.edu/reagan-evil-empire-speech-text/,* accessed 3/5/2014.

[4] *http://www.britannica.com/blogs/2011/02/*

reagan%E2%80%99s-%E2%80%9Cevil-empire%E2%80%9D-speech/,* accessed 3/5/2014.

[5] "Analysis of 20,000 mass grave sites by the DC-Cam Mapping Program and Yale University indicate at least 1,386,734 victims of execution. Estimates of the total number of deaths resulting from Khmer Rouge policies, including disease and starvation, range from 1.7 to 2.5 million out of a 1975 population of roughly 8 million" (*http://en.wikipedia.org/wiki/Killing_Fields*).

[6] Quoted by D. A. Carson in *The Intolerance of Tolerance*, 129.

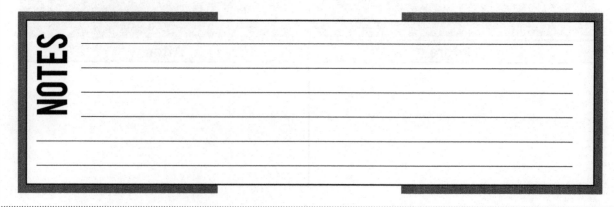

NOTES

the language of evil has been dropped from contemporary moral and ethical discourse."[7]

In the public media, morality is being defined by secularists – those who reject the Bible as a standard of authority because they have generally rejected God. So moral standards are whatever the elite define them to be. The tool of political correctness is being used to enforce its moral values. There is an arbitrary *selective enforcement* of moral values. The media elite decided to oppose smoking. The cigarette companies were compelled to pay the Federal Government millions of dollars, cigarette smoking was removed from movies, and tax dollars are used to pay for advertising against smoking. But, why not go after the evil effects of alcohol? The elite make *arbitrary decisions* about what should be enforced. For example, if the elite decide that homosexuality is an alternate lifestyle equally right as heterosexuality, then anyone who calls it sinful or even deviant behavior is a target for the media who are enforcing political correctness. If the person who says homosexuality is evil is a public figure, his career will probably be destroyed by these powerful forces.[8] Make no

mistake about it. The distance between using pressure from the "politically correct" and using physical force – fines, incarceration, and capital punishment – is but a small step.

How does one determine truth in a secular state without absolute moral values? States without a foundation of absolute truth are forced to stabilize their society by assuming the role of establisher of shared values. D. A. Carson wrote, "In order to maintain stability, governments may be tempted to arrogate more and more authority to themselves (since there are fewer and fewer shared values and norms)."[9] If righteousness and justice are relative terms, then the ones occupying positions of power define what is righteous and just. "Whoever has the most votes, or the most power, or the biggest guns, decides what's right. Might makes right."[10]

Is It Better?

The elitist secularists believe that they are creating a better society by freeing mankind from Christianity. We have witnessed the effect of this movement in such areas as the following: easy divorce and remarriage, sexual liberation, abortion rights, homosexuality, separation of church and state, greed, fatherless homes, vile language, lascivious entertainment, violence, murder, etc. The movement has had its effect on our society for well over fifty years. It seems that enough time has passed that one can legitimately ask, "How well is this philosophy working?" Let's look at the evidence.

William Bennett wrote a book entitled *The Index of Leading Cultural Indicators: American*

---

[7] *http://www.nytimes.com/2002/10/05/books/defining-evil-in-the-wake-of-9-11.html,* accessed 3/5/2014.

[8] For example, President George W. Bush nominated Dr. James W. Holsinger, Jr. as Surgeon General. He drew criticism "from gay rights groups, physicians and lawmakers who say they are troubled by opinions critical of homosexuality that Dr. Holsinger has voiced in nearly 20 years as a high-ranking layman in the United Methodist Church." "The critics said they were worried that Dr. Holsinger might not serve gay men and lesbians fairly as surgeon general, the nation's chief health educator, largely because of a report he wrote in 1991 for a United Methodist committee that essentially described male homosexuality as unnatural" (*http://www.nytimes.com/2007/06/09/washington/09surgeon.html?_r=0*). As a result, Bush

withdrew the nomination. (Incident is taken from D.A. Carson's *The Intolerance of Tolerance,* 134.)

[9] *The Gagging of God*, 17.

[10] S. D. Gaede, *When Tolerance Is No Virtue*, 47.

Society at the End of the 20th Century (1999). He observed,

> Since 1960, our population has increased by 48 percent. But since 1960, even *taking into account* recent improvements, we have seen a 467 percent increase in violent crime, a 463 percent increase in the number of state and federal prisoners; a 461 percent increase in out-of-wedlock births; more than a 200 percent increase in the percentage of children living in single-parent homes; more than a doubling in the teenage suicide rate; a more than 150 percent increase in the number of Americans receiving welfare payments; an almost tenfold increase in the number of cohabiting couples; a doubling of the divorce rate; and a drop of almost 60 points on SAT scores. Since 1973, there have been more than 35 million abortions, increasing from 744,060 in 1973 to 1,365,700 in 1996.[11]

Violence is increasing as evidenced by the bombing of the Alfred P. Murrah Federal Building on April 19, 1995 which killed 168 and injured 680, school shootings,[12] murders,[13] etc. There is a world wide AIDS epidemic.[14]

---

[11] William Bennett, *The Index of Leading Cultural Indicators: American Society at the End of the 20th Century*, 4.

[12] See *http://en.wikipedia.org/wiki/List_of_school_shootings_in_the_United_States* (accessed 3/5/2014) for a list of school shootings from the 18th-21st centuries. Between December 2012 and February 13, 2013, 44 school shootings had happened following the Newtown, CT shooting (*http://www.washingtonpost.com/blogs/answer-sheet/wp/2014/02/13/at-least-44-school-shootings-since-newtown-new-analysis/*, accessed 3/5/2014).

[13] For the year 2013, here are the number murdered in the following cities: New York City – 334; Chicago – 421; Los Angeles – 573; Houston – 214; Dallas – 137; Indianapolis – 142.

[14] The World Health Organization estimates 1.7 million died of AIDS-related illnesses worldwide in 2011 (*http://*

Those of us who are older can provide personal experience regarding how much more violent our country has become during our lifetimes. Most of us grew up in a predominantly Christian culture in which we rarely locked the doors when we left our homes, left the cars unlocked while we shopped (and the windows rolled down so that the car would not be so hot when we returned), and murders were rare. In the 1960s, racial unrest erupted in our nation. The assassination of President John F. Kennedy was so shocking that, even fifty years later, each of us remembers what we were doing when the news of his death came. Indeed, fifty years into the secularist movement, one can see its rotten fruits.

Paul could have been describing American society at the end of the twentieth century, rather than the first century, when he wrote,

> For the wrath of God is revealed from heaven against all ungodliness and unrighteousness of men, who suppress the truth in unrighteousness, because what may be known of God is manifest in them, for God has shown it to them. For since the creation of the world His invisible attributes are clearly seen, being understood by the things that are made, even His eternal power and Godhead, so that they are without excuse, because, although they knew God, they did not glorify Him as God, nor were thankful, but became futile in their thoughts, and their foolish hearts were darkened. Professing to be wise, they became fools, and changed the glory of the incorruptible God into an image made like corruptible man – and birds and four-footed animals and creeping things. Therefore God also gave them up to uncleanness, in the lusts of their hearts, to dishonor their bodies among themselves, who exchanged the truth of God for the lie, and worshiped and served the creature rather than the Creator, who is blessed forever.

---

www.who.int/gho/hiv/epidemic_status/deaths/en/, accessed 3/5/2014).

NOTES

_____

_____

_____

_____

_____

_____

Amen. For this reason God gave them up to vile passions. For even their women exchanged the natural use for what is against nature. Likewise also the men, leaving the natural use of the woman, burned in their lust for one another, men with men committing what is shameful, and receiving in themselves the penalty of their error which was due. And even as they did not like to retain God in their knowledge, God gave them over to a debased mind, to do those things which are not fitting; being filled with all unrighteousness, sexual immorality, wickedness, covetousness, maliciousness; full of envy, murder, strife, deceit, evil-mindedness; they are whisperers, backbiters, haters of God, violent, proud, boasters, inventors of evil things, disobedient to parents, undiscerning, untrustworthy, unloving, unforgiving, unmerciful; who, knowing the righteous judgment of God, that those who practice such things are deserving of death, not only do the same but also approve of those who practice them (Rom. 1:18-32).

This text emphasizes that rejection of God as one's Lord leads inevitably to moral deterioration. Three times in these verses, the text says, "God gave them up" (1:24, 26, 28), indicating that God's divine judgment against rejecting Him as God is to deliver mankind over to his own moral depravity. As we see the immorality and subsequent violence increasing in our country, we should be able to recognize that God is giving us up to our own ungodliness, even as He did early Roman society.

Conclusion

The first purpose of this lesson has been to emphasize that a country or individual who rejects God's word as the revelation of truth is left without a means of determining truth. The result is that the one who has the most votes and most power will determine what is enforced in American society, without regard to what God's word teaches. The enforcement of the values the government decides to impose on our society may include loss of rights, fines, incarceration, or capital punishment. The "political correctness police" are but a few steps removed from using fines and incarceration to enforce their values.

The second purpose of this lesson is to raise the question of how well the secular value system is working in American society. What impact has it had on our culture? Are we better off today than before the Christian value system was rejected? In answer to this question, Romans 1:18-32 was cited to show the relationship between the rejection of the gospel and the increase in immorality.

Questions

1. What is "truth" (John 17:17)? _____

   _____

2. If one rejects God's word as truth, how else may he decide what is right and wrong?_____

   _____

3. In the absence of God's word, who defines what is evil? _____

   _____

NOTES
_____
_____
_____
_____
_____
_____

4. What is "political correctness"?_____
   _____

5. How does "political correctness" enforce its values? _____
   _____

6. What point is being made in the "Is It Better?" section of this lesson? _____
   _____

7. What does Paul teach in Romans 1:18-32 about ...

   a. Why men reject the gospel _____

   _____

   b. Homosexuality _____

   _____

   c. The relationship between rejecting the gospel and immorality _____

   _____

NOTES
_____
_____
_____
_____
_____
_____

The Privatization of Faith

We have all seen it happen. A candidate with a conservative religious background is running for office. He is obviously a good man with strong religious convictions. A reporter asks him a question with the intention of getting him to talk about his views on abortion, with the obvious intent of provoking him to say something that can be used against his campaign. If the candidate opposes abortion, he is perceived as a threat to a woman's right to chose to have an abortion at any stage in her pregnancy. His statement of his beliefs about abortion becomes a front page article in the newspaper and the headline news event at the six o'clock news. The news story may be accurately reported or twisted into something that the candidate never intended. The story may even be picked up by the national news outlets – TV, radio, newspaper, etc. The man's viability as a candidate is over, which was the intent of the liberal slanted reporters at the outset.

The message that is being sent out is that people of faith must keep their convictions to themselves; they are not suitable citizens to be involved in the affairs of state because their religious convictions may influence their political decisions. The effect is that people of faith are second-class citizens. Everyone is welcomed in the public square – people of all races, religious people with liberal views, people from all religious backgrounds – Muslim, Hindu, Buddhist, agnostic, atheist, etc. – except Christians! Bible believing citizens are told in no uncertain terms that they need to keep their religious convictions to themselves. Significantly, secularists/humanists/atheists do not live by the same standard. They are encouraged to discuss openly their religious convictions and make political decisions drawn from their religious worldview.

How did we get to the point that faith must be kept private?

How Faith Became Privatized

One of the reasons that faith was pushed to the realm of opinion was that it cannot be proven like scientific facts could be. Water can be heated to 212° and it will boil; the experiment can be repeated in any country by any group of scientists and it will produce the same results. Faith is not able to be subjected to such tests. D. A. Carson explained how faith became privatized as follows:

It is not surprising, then, that toward the end of the nineteenth century and well into the twentieth, science was often associated with positivism in epistemology. Indeed, scientific knowledge became the model for all knowledge:

Before and After

How would you react?

John spoke to his neighbor about coming to church with him. The neighbor was visibly upset that someone was imposing his religion on another and told John to keep his religion to himself.

Before	After

data had to be obtained empirically, or they were suspect. Meanwhile religion, relegated to the category of mere opinion, was necessarily based on "faith." Such "faith" was assumed to be making a bogus claim if it pretended to knowledge, which of course had to be empirically based. "Faith" was merely a privatized opinion. It had little to do with the public arena, and less and less claim on public learning or morals. It could be judged pious and even beneficial only if it remained private, a personal opinion, and in that guise seemed to exercise some socially useful influence in a person's life; it would be denounced as narrow and bigoted if it claimed universal application. Faith must be made subject to reason. "Reason must be our last judge and guide in everything," wrote Locke. Locke's views on the relationship between faith and reason were complex and nuanced (he certainly did not want reason to be entirely freestanding). But his dictum was influential. Others ran with it, and where "reason" is then connected, not with logic and coherence, but with empiricism, faith is progressively squeezed to the peripheral and the private.[1]

Because science can be subjected to empirical tests, scientific knowledge was deemed more reliable than religious faith.[2] Secularists "regularly view their position as morally neutral and therefore as intrinsically superior, so that that position *ought* to be supported by law, even if it means suppressing, by law, those who contest this view."[3]

Added to this, one must also notice how Protestant religion has contributed to the

privatization of faith. In the mid-twentieth century, bumper stickers were on many cars that said, "Attend the Church of Your Choice!" The idea was that it did not matter where you go to church, just so long as you go. There was but a small step from "Attend the *Church* of Your Choice!" to the mosque, synagogue, or any other place of worship. So long as one worships *a god*, it does not matter which one he worships. There was but another small step to "choose the lifestyle of your choice" (heterosexual/homosexual). In the twenty-first century, even active members of churches with highly defined doctrine have developed the attitude of personalizing their faith. They go through the Bible and their creed books, as they go through a cafeteria line, picking and choosing what appeals to them, creating their own personal faith. What is one person's faith has little or no relevance for another person. Therefore, he should just keep his faith to himself.

It has become an invasion of private space for one person to speak to another person about his faith. Even visitors to worship services are protective of their privacy, not preferring a visit from the preacher until they initiate it.

Keeping Religion out of the Public Square

We will say more about the separation of church and state later, but the privatization of faith also means that faith should not be the basis for making political decisions.[4] Writing about separation of church and state, Carson also said,

---

[1] D. A. Carson, *The Gagging of God*, 63.

[2] Many other areas of knowledge could not be subjected to the scientific method, such as history, psychology, sociology, anthropology, literature, etc. But these have not been devalued in the same way as has religious knowledge.

[3] D. A. Carson, *The Intolerance of Tolerance*, 88.

---

[4] This idea is not universally applied. Those with a secular and liberal religious faith are welcomed to the table for discussion of political decisions. The assumption is that the faith of the secularists and liberals is superior or even religiously neutral. Although post-modernism teaches that all value judgments are

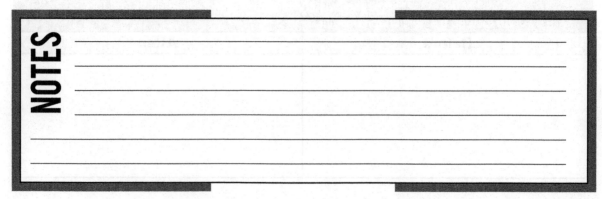

NOTES

One of the effects, for good and ill, of the varied developments regarding the relationships between church and state is the almost inevitable and certainly incessant pressure to restrict religion to private domains. We start by insisting that the state can neither establish nor prohibit religion, and agree that, reciprocally, religion does not have the right to control the state. Then in a mighty bound many infer further that religion does not have the right to influence any of the decisions of the state, and therefore conclude that religion must be restricted to a small and privatized world or the great barrier between church and state is jeopardized.[5]

The process of "secularization may squeeze religion away from the public sectors of politics, the media, and the academic world, into the purely private sectors. By some assessments, a nation may become more secularized and more religious at the same time. It's just that the religious side does not matter very much anymore in the public square and therefore in the direction of the nation, in its public pulse."[6] Carson continued,

> The switch that these cultural developments have flipped lies in the domain of presuppositions. Until the early part of the nineteenth century, the overwhelming majority of people in Europe and of European descent presupposed the existence of God. That meant that questions about tolerance and intolerance had to be worked out within the framework of this presupposition, within the framework of what people thought about God. By the end of the century, however, a cultural switch was flipped: either people did not presuppose the existence of God, or, if they did, they no longer presupposed that he was immediately

equally valid, obviously some value judgments are more valid than others!

[5] D. A. Carson, *The Intolerance of Tolerance*, 66-67.

[6] *Ibid.*, 71.

relevant to all the questions raised in the public square. That in turn meant that questions about tolerance and intolerance had to be worked out within grids that were either non-theistic or whose theism was so attenuated by the rising forces of secularization that they exercised little control.[7]

More and more religion is being pushed out of our public institutions. School prayer "is unconstitutional if it coerces students to participate in a religious activity, or if it indicates a state endorsement of religion."[8] A school can require a teacher to remove the Bible and Christian literature from his classroom library and prohibit him from reading the Bible during silent reading time in class.[9] The Ten Commandments cannot be posted in a public school classroom; posting it on any public property has had conflicting rulings.[10] To many people, religion is just irrelevant.

Evangelism Becomes a Dirty Word

As religion is being pushed further and further from the open forum of the public square and

---

[7] Carson, *op. cit.*, 71-72.

[8] See summary from American Center for Law and Justice, *http://media.aclj.org/pdf/school-prayer-full-memos.pdf*, p. 2 (accessed 3/8/2014). However, any student initiated prayer is not only permissible, but constitutionally protected.

[9] McDowell and Hostetler, 18.

[10] See the 1980 *Stone v. Graham* decision that prohibits them being placed in the classroom; the *McCreary v. ACLU of Kentucky* decision prohibited their display in the county courthouse, although the *Van Orden v. Perry* decision allowed their display in the Texas capitol grounds. For a summary of the issue from a secularist perspective see *http://archive.adl.org/10comm/print.html*, accessed 3/8/2014.

NOTES

treated as private, the work of evangelism is being threatened. The effort to persuade others to accept one's faith is subtly becoming an evil; it is "proselytizing." Here is their thinking:

> One of the objectionable customs of many religions especially most theistic ones is proselytization. I consider this practice rude and condescending because of its implication that the adherent's beliefs are superior to those of other people's and thus they need to be saved from the error of their ways.[11]

> The apparent contradiction seems to be resolved because evangelical Christians imagine themselves to be superior to others in the sense of having access to privileged information. They adopt a paternalistic attitude: their actions may be perceived in a negative fashion, but because they know so much better than others, this is a price worth paying in order to rescue people from their own sinfulness.[12]

This attitude is not confined to agnostics and atheists; those who are members of various denominations view with disdain anyone who would try to persuade them to leave their denomination for another church. "Some Christians define 'proselytism' more narrowly as the attempt to convert people from one Christian tradition to another; those who use the term in this way generally view the practice as illegitimate and in contrast to evangelism, which is converting non-Christians to Christianity."[13]

---

[11] "The Condescending Nature of Proselytizing," December 11, 2012 post on the *Atheist Revolution* web site: *http://www.atheistrev.com/2012/12/the-condescending-nature-of.html*, accessed 3/8/2014.

[12] "Why Do Atheists Object to Evangelism & Proselytization?" by Austin Cline, posted on *About Agnosticism/Atheism* web site (*http://atheism.about.com/od/atheismatheiststheism/a/ObjectEvangeliz.htm*, accessed 3/8/2014).

[13] "Proselytism," *http://en.wikipedia.org/wiki/*

Given these attitudes, the Christian is faced with addressing how to obey the Lord's command to evangelize in a world which privatizes faith.

The Lord gave His disciples the charge to take the gospel to the entire world.

> And Jesus came and spoke to them, saying, "All authority has been given to Me in heaven and on earth. Go therefore and make disciples of all the nations, baptizing them in the name of the Father and of the Son and of the Holy Spirit, teaching them to observe all things that I have commanded you; and lo, I am with you always, even to the end of the age" (Matt. 28:18-20).

> And He said to them, "Go into all the world and preach the gospel to every creature. He who believes and is baptized will be saved; but he who does not believe will be condemned" (Mark 16:15-16).

The Lord charged His Apostles to be His witnesses throughout the world saying, "But you shall receive power when the Holy Spirit has come upon you; and you shall be witnesses to Me in Jerusalem, and in all Judea and Samaria, and to the end of the earth" (Acts 1:8).

The implications of the Great Commission are as follows: (a) All men are lost in sin (Rom. 3:23); (b) Jesus is the only atonement for sin (Matt. 26:28; John 14:6; Acts 4:12); (c) The gospel should be taken to all men in order that they can be saved from their sins (Rom. 1:16). So, the disciples went out preaching salvation through Jesus Christ. Early disciples did not think that one could be saved by being a Pharisee, Sadducee, Essene, Herodian, or any other Jewish sect. They did not think that one could be saved by being a Samaritan, so the gospel had to be taken to Samaria as well (Acts 8:5-26; cf. John 4). And certainly mankind

---

Proselytism, accessed 3/8/2014.

NOTES

_____

_____

_____

_____

_____

_____

could not be saved worshiping other gods, so the gospel had to be taken to pagan religions. When Paul preached at Athens, he said, "Truly, these times of ignorance God overlooked, but now commands all men everywhere to repent, because He has appointed a day on which He will judge the world in righteousness by the Man whom He has ordained. He has given assurance of this to all by raising Him from the dead" (Acts 17:30-31).

In preaching the gospel on pagan soils, the disciples "turned the world upside down" (Acts 17:6). Those at Ephesus who made their living selling statues of Diana were troubled by Paul's preaching.

> For a certain man named Demetrius, a silversmith, who made silver shrines of Diana, brought no small profit to the craftsmen. He called them together with the workers of similar occupation, and said: "Men, you know that we have our prosperity by this trade. Moreover you see and hear that not only at Ephesus, but throughout almost all Asia, this Paul has persuaded and turned away many people, saying that they are not gods which are made with hands. So not only is this trade of ours in danger of falling into disrepute, but also the temple of the great goddess Diana may be despised and her magnificence destroyed, whom all Asia and the world worship" (Acts 19:24-27).

These Ephesians correctly understood Paul's preaching: "they are not gods which are made with hands" and that idolatry is sinful. Paul's work was to convert people. Writing to the Thessalonians, Paul explained his work: "For they themselves declare concerning us what manner of entry we had to you, and *how you turned to God from idols to serve the living and true God, and to wait for His Son from heaven, whom He raised from the dead*, even Jesus who delivers us from the wrath to come" (1 Thess. 1:9-10).

However, in the twenty-first century, post-modernism teaches that all religions are equally valid so trying to convert a person from one religion to another, to proselytize, is morally wrong.[14] This view of evangelism, or proselytizing, makes converting the lost more difficult. Evangelism has now become a dirty word, a sign of a "bad" (another value judgment!) religion.

Conclusion

As was the case in the first century, the Lord's people are compelled to obey the Lord rather than comply with the values of the age in which they live. Far from keeping our faith to ourselves, we must preach it – "in season and out of season" (2 Tim. 4:2). If we preach the word to one who has no interest in it, we must "shake off the dust of your feet" and move on to those who might be willing to listen (Matt. 10:14). Not even the Lord found every soul willing to obey His word, nor should we expect that we will. The attitudes toward the gospel are not the same in every social climate and culture. Some cultures are more interested in the gospel than others are. Unfortunately, America is less attracted to the Lord's gospel than it formerly was. So what do we do?

When I was a lad, my Dad and I fished whenever we had opportunity. Sometimes we fished when the fish would bite everything we put on our hooks. Sometimes we fished when they

---

[14] How can proselytizing be wrong unless there is some absolute standard by which to measure all things? According to the principles of post-modernism, proselytizing may be wrong for one person but not for another. The one who thinks proselytizing is wrong should keep his secular religion to himself!

NOTES
_____
_____
_____
_____
_____
_____

would not bite anything we put on our hooks. If we wanted to eat fish on those days, we had to work a lot harder at fishing. The same is true about fishing for men. The words God spoke to the prophet Ezekiel seem particularly relevant to describe preaching in America in the twenty-first century:

> Then He said to me: "Son of man, go to the house of Israel and speak with My words to them. For you are not sent to a people of unfamiliar speech and of hard language, but to the house of Israel, not to many people of unfamiliar speech and of hard language, whose words you cannot understand. Surely, had I sent you to them, they would have listened to you. But the house of Israel will not listen to you, because they will not listen to Me; for all the house of Israel are impudent and hard-hearted. Behold, I have made your face strong against their faces, and your forehead strong against their foreheads. Like adamant stone, harder than flint, I have made your forehead; do not be afraid of them, nor be dismayed at their looks, though they are a rebellious house." Moreover He said to me: "Son of man, receive into your heart all My words that I speak to you, and hear with your ears. And go, get to the captives, to the children of your people, and speak to them and tell them, 'Thus says the Lord GOD,' whether they hear, or whether they refuse" (Ezek. 3:4-11).

Questions

1. Is the workbook description of how religiously conservative candidates for public office are treated in the public media the same as your own assessment? Cite an example to support your opinion.
   _____
   _____

2. Name some commonly held truth on various topics of study that cannot be subjected to the scientific method of experimentation. _____
   _____

3. How is "faith" being squeezed out of the public arena? _____
   _____

4. Why is secular humanism considered objective or religiously neutral, whereas those opposing secular humanism are asked to keep their religious beliefs to themselves? _____
   _____

5. How does choosing one's own personal faith relate to faith being privatized?_____
   _____

6. How does the privatization of faith affect evangelism?_____
   _____

7. How has religion been removed from public institutions?_____
   _____

8. Why is evangelism viewed as wrong by some people today? _____
   _____

9. What beliefs underlie the Great Commission? _____
   _____

10. Why did the early church think that teaching others the gospel is a good work? _____
   _____

Separation of Church and State (1)

The privatization of faith not only has affected evangelism, resulting in people feeling uncomfortable when being approached by a Christian who is trying to evangelize his neighbor, it has also resulted in an effort to drive religion from the public square (i.e., public events, political discussions and decisions, etc.). Almost everyone is welcome to discuss the issues of modern society: all races of people Native Americans, Blacks, Caucasians, Hispanics (both legal and illegal immigrants), immigrants for all countries, most religions (Christians with a liberal perspective, Islamists, Buddhists, Hinduists, atheists, etc.), all adult age groups (Generations X, Y, Z), all economic levels, etc. The "diversity" is perceived to be an important contribution to making decisions affecting all Americans; every participant brings his belief system and values which shape and define his perspective into the public square. However, those who are religious conservatives are not welcome in the public square. Every time a conservative becomes vocal in expressing his convictions, the media begins to question how his faith will influence his politics, as though only Christians allow their faith to influence their political beliefs! The common justification for excluding religious conservatives is that the Constitution demands the separation of church and state.

What should be the relationship of church and state in the New Testament era? This lesson will briefly review the history of the issue of church and state in America, show how the secular agenda that predominates modern society views religion as a threat, and then suggest some relationships which church and state have developed that are fundamentally flawed.

The Background for the First Amendment to the United States Constitution

The background of the first settlers in America significantly influenced their concepts of the relationship between church and state. Many of them had come from countries that had a state church that used the arm of civil government as a tool to punish dissenters. However, those who had been victims of the Spanish Inquisition, for example, were not so much opposed to a state church existing as they were to which church controlled the state. They were opposed to the Roman Catholic Church using the civil state to punish dissenters or heretics; however, when these dissenters separated from the Catholic Church, they created a similar partnership between Protestant churches and the civil state. For example, in Geneva, Switzerland,

Before and After	
What is wrong with this?	
A church in a ghetto provides day care services and a school for poor children where free lunches are served. They receive government funds to pay for these services.	
Before	**After**

John Calvin denounced Michael Servetus for his heretical views, resulting in his execution on October 27, 1553.[1] The civil wars in France between the Huguenots and the Catholics resulted in thousands of deaths. The Puritans fled to America to escape severely restrictive laws against their religion in England. But, when these persecuted people came to America, some wanted to establish a new state church – one which they controlled.

Drawing from this background, the first amendment to the United States Constitution restricted the rights of the Federal Government with respect to religion. Here is the First Amendment:

> Congress shall make no law respecting an establishment of religion, or prohibiting the free exercise thereof; or abridging the freedom of speech, or of the press; or the right of the people peaceably to assemble, and to petition the government for a redress of grievances.

The First Amendment was an advance in protecting the liberties of minority religions. The state government could not be used to force anyone to worship or to worship in a way that he did not personally believe was acceptable to God. However, the wording of the First Amendment left plenty of room for future conflict: What is included in "establishing" a religion? May a principal read a Scripture and lead a public prayer at the beginning of a school day? Does public prayer at a football game (a government sponsored event on government premises) constitute a violation of the First Amendment? Does refusing to allow a valedictorian to express her convictions about God in her valedictory address violate her right to free speech?

---

[1] *http://en.wikipedia.org/wiki/Michael_Servetus.*

The Separation of Church and State

The media speak so much of the "separation of church and state" that one might think it is enshrined in the Constitution; however, the words are not found in the U.S. Constitution. The concept of the separation of church and state had to be worked out at a later time. Roger Williams was a leading voice in advocating that the Scriptures did not authorize a state church, thus concluding that these two institutions should be separate. He did not think that the state had the right to force anyone to worship or to worship in any particular manner. However, the phrase "wall of separation between church and state" was first used by President Thomas Jefferson. Bill McCarthy explained when and how that happened as follows:

> In 1801, the Danbury Baptist Association of Danbury, Connecticut, heard a rumor that the Congregationalist denomination was about to be made the national denomination. That rumor distressed the Danbury Baptists, as it should have. Consequently, they fired off a letter to President Thomas Jefferson voicing their concern. On January 1, 1802, Jefferson wrote the Danbury Baptists, assuring them that "the First Amendment has erected a wall of separation between church and state."[2]

---

[2] His exact quote was this: "Believing with you that religion is a matter which lies solely between Man & his God, that he owes account to none other for his faith or his worship, that the legitimate powers of government reach actions only, & not opinions, I contemplate with sovereign reverence that act of the whole American people which declared that their legislature should 'make no law respecting an establishment of religion, or prohibiting the free exercise thereof,' thus building *a wall of separation between Church & State*" ["Jefferson's Letter to the Danbury Baptists." U.S. Library of Congress, Retrieved 2006-11-31] (*http://en.wikipedia.org/wiki/Separation_of_church_and_*

NOTES
_____
_____
_____
_____
_____
_____

His letter explained that they need not fear the establishment of a national denomination – and that while the wall of the First Amendment would protect the church from government control – there always would be open and free religious expression of all orthodox religious practices, for true religious duties would never threaten the purpose of government. The (sic; probably "that") government would interfere with a religious activity was a direct menace to the government or to the overall peace and good order of society. (Later Supreme Court identified potential "religious" activities in which the government might interfere: things like human sacrifice, bigamy or polygamy, the advocation of immorality or licentiousness, etc. If any of these activities were to occur in the name of "religion," then the government would interfere, for these were activities which threaten public peace and safety; but with orthodox religious practices, the government would not interfere.)[3]

Jefferson's statement later became incorporated into American law through the courts. D. A. Carson explains how this occurred:

... in the context of his letter to the Baptists of Connecticut, the President's (Thomas Jefferson) purpose was to defend the free exercise of religion, rather than ban it to the private sphere. Moreover, as is well known, Jefferson ended this missive with a prayer, responding in kind to the Baptists' prayer for him. But whatever Jefferson meant, the First Amendment was increasingly seen through the grid of that phrase. It entered the vocabulary of the Supreme Court in 1878 (*Reynolds v. United States*), though probably it played little if any role in the decision. The climax came in the landmark case *Everson v. Board of Education* (1947), in which Justice

Hugo L. Black, writing the majority opinion and citing no precedent other than *Reynolds*, famously argued that in the words of Jefferson, the First Amendment *itself* has erected "'a wall of separation between Church and State.'... That wall must be kept high and impregnable. We could not approve the slightest breach."[4]

Assessing the significance of the "wall of separation between Church and State," Kevin Pybas, from Missouri State University, observed, "Because neither the ratification history of the First Amendment nor the plain language of it provides straightforward answers to questions of religious liberty, the Court is relatively free to define the scope of religious liberty along lines it believes most advantageous to the nation."[5] *What this means is that the First Amendment means whatever the nine justices on the Supreme Court rule that it should mean!*

Interpreting the First Amendment

The First Amendment ("Congress shall make no law respecting an establishment of religion, or prohibiting the free exercise thereof") has two points that are the crux of the discussion of church and state issues: (a) Congress shall make no laws respecting an establishment of religion; (b) Congress shall make no laws prohibiting the free exercise thereof. Depending upon his view of religion, a justice will take different stances toward church and state. The four ways to look at religion are: "1) 'dangerous quasi-governments in need of restraint'; 2) 'valuable private associations needing autonomy

state#cite_note-Jefferson11-15, accessed 3/10/2014; italics added by mw).

[3] Fr. Bill McCarthy, "Not Separation of God from State," *http://www.freerepublic.com/focus/news/987191/posts*, accessed 3/10/2014.

[4] D. A. Carson, *Christ and Culture Revisited*, 174-175.

[5] Kevin Pybas, "Religious Groups in a Free Society," presented at the Paul B. Henry Institute Symposium on Religion and Politics at Calvin College, April 23-25, 2009, p. 3.

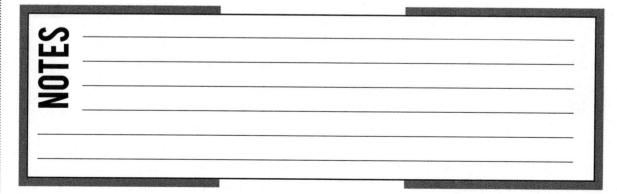

NOTES

Views of Religious groups	Enforcement of Free Exercise Clause	Enforcement of Establishing Clause	Social Vision
Quasi-governments	weak	strong	secularism
Valuable private associations	strong	strong	separationism
Discrete and insular minorities	strong	weak	accommodationism
Ordinary interest groups	weak	weak	assimilationism

but not public subsidy'; 3) 'discrete and insular minorities in need of both equal treatment and affirmative action' and 4) 'ordinary interest groups whose gains or losses in the political process may be expected to even out along with others' over time."[6] Constitutional scholars break down into four groups according to Pybas as provided in his chart (above)[7]:

In recent years, the secularist position ("quasi-governments") has predominated,[8]

which emphasizes a weak enforcement of the free exercise of religion clause and a strong enforcement of the establishment clause. The secularist view of religion understands religion "in mostly negative terms and thus seeks to minimize the public influence of religion."[9] Here is the secularist view of the threat of religion:

> On this account of religious groups, their ability, unique among private associations, "to interpret the world and express shared understandings, and to command deep allegiance, fidelity, and obedience from their adherents" brings them into competition with the state for the loyalty of their adherents. Religious groups "exert a quasi-sovereign authority over their members, posting a potential rivalry with the state when religious and secular obligations conflict." Unlike other voluntary associations, religious organizations can supply "a totalistic worldview that colors not only family and charitable life, but also all of an individual's social relationships, potentially dividing people along deep lines, with religious conflict etched in ancient grievances passed down across generations." Consequently, religious groups

---

[6] *Ibid.*, 4. This breakdown is credited to Kathleen Sullivan, *The New Religion and the Constitution,* 116 *Harvard Law Review* 1397 (2003).

[7] *Op. cit.*, 7.

[8] Kathleen M. Sullivan emphasized that the "freedom of religion" implies also the "freedom from religion" and that government's non-establishment clause leads to the government establishment of a secularist state. She writes, "Just as the free exercise of religion implies the free exercise of non-religion, so the ban on establishment of religion establishes a civil public order, which ends the war of all sects against all. The price of this truce is *the banishment of religion from the public square* (emphasis mine, mw), but the reward should be allowing religious subcultures to withdraw from regulation insofar as compatible with peaceful diarchic coexistence" ["Religion and Liberal

Democracy," *University of Chicago Law Review* 59 (Winter, 1992), 195-223].

[9] Pybas, 8.

NOTES

_____
_____
_____
_____
_____
_____

"threaten to become normative enclaves outside of and apart from secular society, even quasi-governments – separatist communities with distinctive epistemic perspectives and the power to command obedience anchored in faith, posing a danger that they will become sovereign rivals to the state, or even seedbeds for terrorism, separatism, and revolt."[10, 11]

Pybas summarized this approach to the First Amendment:

> For Supreme Court justices and others who believe that the social impact of religion is mainly harmful, it follows that they would advance an interpretation of the First Amendment that would seek to restrain religion's influence and potential for harm. This is accomplished by denying religion any significant public space. The secularist social vision sees religion as "merely something that people should practice in private without affirmative state support." This is achieved by weakly enforcing the Free Exercise Clause and strongly enforcing the Establishment Clause.[12]

The animus toward religion can be seen in whether or not religious activities are given equal access to public facilities and government funding as other organizations. For example,

if a university provides funds to publish all student publications, must it also provide funds to publish those publications sent out by student religious groups? Nelson Tebbe argues that the state should be allowed considerable latitude to exclude religious activities and actors from its support on the grounds of promoting equal citizenship for members of minority faith (or no faith at all), fostering community accord (because religion is divisive), and respecting taxpayers' freedom of conscience [defined as "the religious freedom of taxpayers who object to supporting institutions with which they differ as a matter of conscience" (as if religious people do not have a conscience about their tax dollars being used for things they oppose, such as state funded schools that are consistently secular or atheistic in their teaching content)].[13] Writing in response to Tebbe, Thomas C. Berg[14] replied that "the state has no power 'to make a value judgment favoring [nonreligion] over [religion]'....It has no power 'pursuant to democratic processes, [to] expres[s] a preference for [nonreligion over religion].'"[15] Government neutrality toward religion should mean that government acts in a way that minimizes its influence over religious choices, not establishing a secular state!

The emphasis on a strong enforcement of the Establishment Clause leads to the view that religious schools and social services should not be able to receive any public funds, even though

---

[10] Pybas, 8-9.

[11] As one reads Pybas' description of the secularists' attitude toward religion, he is reminded of the first-century Roman view that Christianity posed a threat to the Roman Empire. Christians' refusal to bow before the statues of Roman emperors and offer their incense on his altar was interpreted as rebellion against the government and a threat to the unity of the Roman Empire. This is what led to the intermittent persecution of Christians from the late first century through A.D. 325 when Constantine issued the Edict of Milan granting religious liberty to Christians and other religions (see "Edict of Milan," *http://en.wikipedia.org/wiki/Edict_of_Milan*, accessed 3/13/2014).

[12] Pybas, 12.

---

[13] Nelson Tebbe, "Excluding Religion," *University of Pennsylvania Law Review* (May 2008), 1264-1339.

[14] St. Ives Professor of Law and Co-Director of the Murphy Institute for Catholic Thought, Law, and Public Policy.

[15] Berg, "Religious Choice and Exclusions of Religion," *University of St. Thomas (Minnesota) School of Law, Legal Studies Research Paper Series*, PENNumbra (forthcoming 2008), 1-18.

NOTES

they provide the same services that secular organizations which receive federal monies provide. Some religious organizations receive government funds for performing services (for example, funds for textbooks, bus services, medical supplies, etc.).[16] Because religion is viewed as harmful to society, those emphasizing the strong enforcement of the Establishment Clause would insist that religious organizations can receive no assistance from government, either financially or by way of exemptions from applicable laws.

Writing in reaction to the government's animus toward religion, Michael W. McConnell wrote, "The [Supreme] Court's[17] conception of the First Amendment more closely resembled freedom *from* religion (except in its most private manifestations) than freedom *of* religion. The animating principle was not pluralism and diversity, but maintenance of a scrupulous secularism in all aspects of public life touched by government."[18] McConnell continued, "More significant was the Court's tendency to press relentlessly in the direction of a more secular society. The Court's opinion seems to view religion as an unreasoned, aggressive, exclusionary, and divisive force that must be confined to the private sphere. ... The Court's more important mission was to protect democratic society from religion."[19]

---

[16] More will be said about government funding of faith-based social services later.

[17] McConnell was describing the Supreme Court under Chief Justices Earl Warren (1953-1969) and Warren Earl Burger (1969-1986).

[18] McConnell, "Religious Participation in Public Programs: Religious Freedom at a Crossroads," *University of Chicago Law Review* (Winter, 1992), 116.

[19] *Ibid.*, 120.

This animus toward religion is the background explanation for judicial decisions and media bias that contributes to the privatization of religion. As mentioned in the introduction, a candidate who expresses his religious conviction about homosexuality and/or abortion is attacked because he is allowing his religion to influence his political beliefs. However, the First Amendment does not make it illegal for a member of Congress to base a political choice on the grounds of his religious beliefs. Michael J. Perry wrote,

> Although the nonestablishment norm that is constitutional bedrock for us Americans forbids government to privilege one or more churches, it does not go so far as to forbid government to take action based on religiously grounded moral belief. No such rule is – no such rule has ever become – part of our constitutional bedrock. Nor does authoritative case law contain any such rule, as Justice Scalia has emphasized:

> Our cases in no way imply that the Establishment Clause forbids legislators merely to act upon their religious convictions. We surely would not strike down a law providing money to feed the hungry or shelter the homeless if it could be demonstrated that, but for the religious beliefs of the legislators, the funds would not have been approved. ... [P]olitical activism by the religiously motivated is part of our heritage.[20]

Church and State: A Biblical Perspective

Churches have had various relationships to civil government throughout church history. Here are some of the relationships that can be easily identified:

---

[20] Michael J. Perry, "Why Political Reliance on Religiously Grounded Morality Does not Violate the Establishment Clause," *William and Mary Law Review* Vol. 42: Iss. 3, art. 3, pp. 663-683.

NOTES
_____
_____
_____
_____
_____
_____

1. *The church can become the tool of the state.* Some historians interpret Constantine's conversion in 324 A.D. as a conversion to Christianity for political reasons, though others believe his conversion was genuine. He saw Christianity as a powerful social movement that could enhance his political aspirations. Most of us have witnessed politicians catering to Christians for the reason of getting their vote in a coming election. When a morally reprobate politician arranges for a media appearance with a nationally known preacher, he is not there seeking moral advice. Were he seeking moral counsel, he would probably do what most of the rest of us do – arrange for a private meeting with someone in whom we have personal confidence and who has established himself as a man of faith. Just as the church should not be used by human institutions as a fund-raising tool, neither should it be used by politicians and the state for vote getting tools.

Black churches have a tradition of being very active in politics. Frederick C. Harris surveyed blacks churches to see their involvement with politicians. Consider the following table:[21]

---

[21] Frederick C. Harris, "Black Churches and Civic Traditions: Outreach, Activism, and the Politics of Public Funding of Faith-Based Ministries" (*http://www.trincoll.edu/depts/csrpl/Charitable%20Choice%20book/Harris.pdf*, p. 148; accessed 3/12/2014). Harris wrote, "... black churches provided the organizational resources to mobilize the new black electorate. Churches provided the physical space for political gatherings, ministers and church members served as delegates to state constitutional conventions and ran for elected office, and news about politics was regularly dissimilated through black pulpits. ... Some churches aligned themselves with political machines, allowing political elites to employ churches as a direct vehicle for black voter mobilization. Political candidates made direct appeals before black congregations and many black ministers endorsed

The Intensity of Church-Based Political Activism among Blacks	
	Yes (%)
Has a member of the clergy or someone in an official position talked about the needs for people to become involved in politics?	63
In the past year, have you heard any discussions of politics at your church or place of worship?	61
Has any national or local leader spoken at a regular religious service?	48
Have you talked to people about political matters at your church or place of worship?	44
Has a member of the clergy or someone in an official position ever suggested that you vote for or against certain candidates in an election?	29

Source: 1992-1993 National Black Politics Survey (N=1,175)

Political candidates have obviously been using Black churches for votes which influence the outcomes of elections. This is not the relationship that God wants His church to have with the government.

The Moral Majority was founded by Jerry Falwell in 1979 and dissolved in the late 1980s after it became part of the Liberty Federation; its financial difficulties eventually led to its dissolution. The Moral Majority was founded to address the moral decay in America through

---

candidates for public office, thereby delivering votes to a preferred candidate" (147).

NOTES
_____
_____
_____
_____
_____
_____
_____

involvement in politics. The movement lasted a brief decade and had only a minimal and short-lived influence. The Christian Coalition, under Ralph Reed, sought to create a sophisticated political machine to influence American politics to the right. His involvement with superlobbyist Jack Abramoff so compromised his Christianity that his influence among Evangelicals was destroyed.[22] Neither Christian individuals nor churches have fared well when they agree to be used as tools of any given political party. Despite all of the energies put into electing conservative Republicans, the Christian right was disappointed that their elected candidates did little or nothing to address their concerns about the cultural shift happening in America.[23] Babcock astutely said, "When Christians on either end of the political spectrum redefine the church as a voting bloc instead of Christ's very body, then we have succumbed to a false wind of doctrine."[24]

2. *The church views its mission to include being involved in politics.* The work that God has given the church to perform is revealed in Scripture: "For we are His workmanship, created in Christ Jesus for good works, *which God prepared beforehand that we should walk in them*" (Eph. 2:10). The early church is a model for what is legitimate church activity, which is: (1) Preaching the gospel to the lost (Rom. 1:16; 1 Cor. 14:23-25); (2) Edifying the saved (Acts 20:32; Eph. 4:11-12); (3) Relieving the needs of the poor among the saints (Acts 2:44; 4:32-37; 6:1; 1 Cor. 16:1-4; 2 Cor. 8-9; etc.); (4) Public worship (Acts 20:7; 1 Cor. 11:16-34; 12-14; James 2:2). What is conspicuously absent from the New Testament is any instruction that the

church should form a political action committee to lobby Rome or that the church should organize and lead marches protesting social inequities. There are many organizations that have been formed to address various social needs of mankind – education (pre-school through college), benevolence (orphan homes, old folks homes, unwed mothers homes), emotional well being (counsellors for emotional and financial well-being), medical needs (free medical clinics for the poor; hospitals; blood banks; etc.). However, the social gospel program is not the mission of the local church. When social reforms become the mission of a church, the costs in funds and personnel are drained from doing what Christ sent the church to do – to preach the saving gospel to the lost.

3. *The church should not be receiving government funds to provide community services.* In recent years, it has become common for Faith-Based social services to be funded by government resources. The argument has been that Faith-Based organizations should have equal standing with secular-based organizations in competing for federal funds; Faith-based organizations should have the same right to feed at the government trough as do secular organizations that provide the same services. To do otherwise is to make citizens of faith second class citizens without the same rights as others. The result of this reasoning has been that some churches are receiving government funds to pay for the social services they provide for the community (outreach services include helping to reform prison inmates, visit hospitals to assist the sick, provide food and clothing for the indigent, build orphanages and nursing homes, pay for burial services, etc.). The media and government have closed their eyes to the "ethics of activist churches and ministers receiving

---

[22] See Michael Babcock, *UnChristian America*, 3-38.

[23] *Ibid.*, 24.

[24] Babcock, *op. cit.*, 60.

NOTES

_____
_____
_____
_____
_____
_____

contracts because of their support of political candidates."[25] Churches that forsake the Biblical parameters for the work of the church and then apply for and receive government funding to pay for these projects become a part of the church/state establishment and are thereby restrained in preaching the Biblical message that the citizens in that state need to hear. The Lord has not authorized these politico/secular entanglements for the church. Furthermore, the one who supplies the money will dictate how it is spent.

Conclusion

This lesson has shown that animus toward religion has moved government to drive religion from participation in the public square – the place where decisions are made

_____

[25] Harris, 150. Harris quotes historian Melvin Holli as saying this about the political machine in Chicago politics: "Federal anti-poverty money was used to keep black churches pro-administration, or at least to keep them from becoming forums for (Richard J.) Daley's opponents" (153). A. Patterson Jackson, the later senior pastor of Liberty Baptist Church, refused to accept funds from the city of Chicago, saying, "We feel that if you accept a favor from a politician one day you will have to pay it back. I know that" (153).

for how government functions. Under the guise of the first amendment's prohibition for government to be involved in establishing a religion, the government has moved toward a state established atheistic religion, much as have Communist countries. State-sponsored secularism is just as certainly a state-sponsored religion as is a state-sponsored church (denomination). The freedom *of* religion clause has become freedom *from* religion in practice.

The church/state relationship has been varied through the centuries. Both the church and state err when the church becomes the tool of the state, when the church becomes a political action committee, and when the government supports churches to do works the Bible never authorized the church to perform (provide day care services, social services of various kinds, etc.). The government that supplies funds to the churches will dictate how the funds can be spent. Furthermore, the politicians who decide which churches to fund will always expect something (votes, political support) in return for their decision to direct funds to that church. This is a perilous relationship that has been used by political machines to entrench their political power base.

Questions

1. What was the common concept of the relationship of church and state in the Reformation era?

_____

2. What are some religious practices that the United States government would use military/police force to prevent. _____

_____

NOTES

_____
_____
_____
_____
_____
_____

3. How does the United States define what the first amendment to the U.S. Constitution means?

_____

_____

4. What are the two defining principles of the First Amendment?

a._____

b._____

5. What is the difference between "freedom of religion" and "freedom from religion"?_____

_____

6. What threat to the state do secularists believe that churches pose? _____

_____

7. How is a government established secular state different from a government established church?

_____

_____

8. Name some countries that have had government established secularism (atheism). _____

_____

_____

9. A Christian, atheist, and Islamist are elected to the Senate. Which one(s) allows his worldviews (religious beliefs) to affect his votes in Congress? _____

_____

10. How can the church become the pawn of politicians?_____

_____

11. What are the legititmate, Bible authorized works that God has given to the church (provide Scripture with their answers)? _____

_____

12. What are some unauthorized works that churches are involved in?_____

_____

13. What dangers are inherent when churches are funded from government resources? _____

_____

NOTES

_____

_____

_____

_____

_____

_____

Separation of Church and State (2)

The relationship between God's people and the political state is the subject of several passages in the New Testament.[1] In most of these, the government is either hostile or, at best, neutral toward Christianity. However, when the subject is expanded to include God's people under the Old Testament, other types of association between God's people and government are seen. In this lesson, we will look at the various relationships that can exist between church and state and search for God's guidance in how to live under various circumstances.

Different Relationships between Church and State

Throughout world history, God's people have been forced to live in a variety of circumstances. We will profit from a consideration of how God's people lived under those circumstances, giving us guidance for how we should live today.

1. Government hostility. There have been times when governments have been hostile to the people of God. The children of Israel, who

---

[1] The New Testament documents cover only 100 years of history of church/state relationships. Some possible relationships between church and state did not exist during that period (for example, when Christians become so dominant that they are in control of government).

had once enjoyed favored status in Egypt, saw their circumstances change drastically and quickly when there arose a new king (dynasty) that "did not know Joseph" (Exod. 1:8). The new pharaoh saw the Israelites as a threat to his administration and was afraid that they would align themselves with Egypt's enemies should the nation be invaded. Therefore, he made Israelites slaves and eventually took such drastic measures that he ordered that all of the male babies be put to death (Exod. 1:15-22). This was not the only time that God's people were under a hostile government. Oppressions repeated themselves throughout the period of the Judges. The Assyrian and Babylonian captivities were difficult times for God's people. Haman threatened Israelites throughout the Persian Empire when his hatred for Mordecai motivated him to plan the slaughter of Jewish citizens (Esth. 3:7-15).

There were times when God's people were persecuted even under Israelite kings. Ahab married Jezebel, the daughter of the king of Zidon. Jezebel imposed the worship of Baal on Israel, intending to make Baalism the established religion in the Northern Kingdom (1 Kings 16:31-33; 18:4, 19). God's people lived under threat of death from their own government during those days.

Before and After	
What should be a Christian's reaction?	
The government rules that your photography business should be fined and closed because of your refusal to photograph the wedding of a gay couple.	
Before	**After**

In the New Testament, Christians suffered from the official Jewish leadership in Jerusalem (Acts 5:40-41), from mob action (the murder of Stephen, Acts 7:54-8:1; attempted murder of Paul, Acts 23:12-35), and from official actions of vassal kings (Herod Agrippa I put James to death and imprisoned Peter with the intention to execute him, Acts 12:1-4). The book of Revelation describes similar government hostility toward Christians (Rev. 2:10, 13; 13:1-10).

2. Sporadic confrontation. Sometimes God's people faced persecution and suffering that were not official acts of State. For example, Paul and Silas were beaten at Philippi after casting out a demon from a woman (Acts 16:16-40). The officials themselves would have been in trouble with their superiors had the incident been investigated. Nevertheless, there were isolated incidences periodically in various cities of the empire (perhaps Rev. 2:6, 14-16 should be understood in this sense). In these cases, the State is not an active agent of persecution, but it certainly is not a defender of freedom of religion.

In references to both circumstances described in sections *1* and *2*, Christians had an allegiance to a power greater than civil government. Peter and John expressed their priority of responsibilities to the Jewish leadership in Jerusalem, when the Jewish authorities ordered them to quit preaching in the name of Jesus. Peter said, "Whether it is right in the sight of God to listen to you more than to God, you judge. For we cannot but speak the things which we have seen and heard" (Acts 4:19-20). A Christian's first loyalty is to God (Matt. 22:37). Jesus Himself had taught them to so order their priorities, "Render therefore to Caesar the things that are Caesar's, and to God the things that are God's" (Matt. 22:21). A Christian's citizenship is in heaven (Phil. 3:20).

3. Government neutrality. Sometimes government is neither actively favoring God's people nor actively hostile toward them. When Joseph's family migrated to Egypt, they were given special treatment because of their relationship to Joseph (Gen. 45:17-20); they were given some of the best land in Egypt (Goshen, 46:28; 47:6) and special jobs (47:6). During the early Persian period, King Cyrus (599-575 B.C.) permitted Israelites to return to their homelands and rebuild the Temple (2 Chron. 36:22-23; Ezra 1:1-4). King Artaxerxes (ruled from 464-424 B.C.) allowed Nehemiah to help rebuild the walls of Jerusalem and even appointed him governor over the province (Neh. 5:14). There have been many periods during which governments have shown a neutrality to God's people. Paul taught Christians to pray that governments would allow Christians to live a quiet and peaceful life (1 Tim. 2:2).

4. God's people administer government. The occasions when God's people have administered government have been relatively rare. However, in the Israelite nation, righteous men sometimes ruled the nation. Remember such great leaders as Moses, Joshua, David, Solomon, Asa, Jehoshaphat, Joash (in his youth), Amaziah (in his youth), Uzziah, Jotham, Hezekiah, and Josiah. Perhaps having the responsibility to govern righteously is a greater burden than living under other situations. Even in the golden years of his reign, Solomon faced difficult decisions in administering justice (two women claiming the same baby, 1 Kings 3:16-28), as also did David (avenging the slaughter of the Gibeonites by the hanging of Saul's sons, 2 Sam. 21:1-11). Despite the glory associated with his forty year reign, Solomon's spending to build up the kingdom left Israelites suffering under such high taxation that a rebellion occurred when his son Rehoboam became the new king (1 Kings 12:4,

NOTES

_____
_____
_____
_____
_____
_____

19). Undoubtedly, however, God's people were able to live peaceable and quiet lives during such administrations.

Perhaps there are other relationships between government and God's people that should be given special attention, but these seem the most obvious.

Circumstances Can Change Swiftly

The relationship between God's people and government is always fluid; the relationship can change slowly or rapidly. The favored status of God's people in Egypt changed when a new dynasty of Pharaohs took control of the country. The Scripture simply says, "Now there arose a new king over Egypt, who did not know Joseph" (Exod. 1:8). The change resulted in the favored people becoming slaves and eventually were ordered to put to death their children. In the Persian period, the anger of Haman, an influential sub-ordinate to King Ahasuerus, resulted in a decree being signed that would have put to death all of the Jews in the Persian Empire (Esth. 3:8-10). Hitler's Final Solution (*die Endlösung*) to systematically exterminate the Jewish people in Nazi-occupied Europe illustrates again how government can be used persecute its own people. The Khmer Rouge regime arrested and eventually executed almost everyone suspected of connections with the former government or with foreign governments, as well as professionals and intellectuals. Ethnic Vietnamese, ethnic Thai, ethnic Chinese, ethnic Cham, Cambodian Christians, and the Buddhist monkhood were the demographic targets of persecution. It is estimated that 1.7 million people were killed under the Khmer Rouge regime. Ethnic cleansing is a term used to describe "the systematic forced removal of ethnic or religious groups from a given territory with the intent of creating a territory inhabited by people of a homogeneous or pure ethnicity, religion, culture, and history." Ethnic cleansing has most recently been used to describe events in the 1990s Bosnian war between the Serbs and Croats when both sides were guilty of atrocities to purge their districts of unwanted citizens.[2]

Recognizing the potentialities for change in governments makes one watch with a wary eye the effects of the cultural revolution in the United States that began in the 1960s and has taken control of government in the United States. Its rejection of the Christian values of the mid-twentieth century is becoming more entrenched in America every year. Michael Babcock wrote, "It can no longer be claimed on demographic grounds that the 'vast majority' of Americans believe in Christ and the gospel. ... Nor are the cultural influences of Christianity any longer 'universal.'"[3] The removal of prayer from public schools in the *Engel v. Vitale* case in 1962 (as well as the removal of religious symbols from public buildings – the removal of the Ten Commandments from the schools and court houses, for example), the enacting of no-fault divorce laws, the "right to choose" abortion law of 1973, and the establishment of gay rights are indicative of this cultural shift. Here are some ominous examples that cause apprehension in America:

- The city of San Jose erected a $500,000 statue of Quetzalcoatl, an Aztec god, while less than a hundred miles away, a 103-foot cross in San Francisco park was determined

[2] Interestingly, America celebrates its ethnic diversity whereas these countries are experiencing agonizing conflicts from alienated sub-cultures. Horrible war crimes of ethnic cleansing have been committed in an effort to create an homogenous society.

[3] Michael Babcock, *Unchristian America*, 50.

NOTES
_____
_____
_____
_____
_____
_____

to be unconstitutional and was slated for destruction.[4]

- Judge Samuel B. Kent of the U.S. District Court for the Southern District of Texas ruled that "any student mentioning the name of Jesus in a graduation prayer would be sentenced to a six-month jail term."[5]

- The *Lee v. Weisman* case "held, for example, that a short, bland, non-sectarian prayer at a public school commencement amounted to a forbidden establishment of religion.[6]

- "During the last ten years there have been attempts to 'derecognize' chapters of InterVarsity Christian Fellowship (IVCF) at Tufts, Harvard, Rutgers, the University of North Carolina, and elsewhere. In each case, the local chapter was charged with being discriminatory, either because it insisted that its officers (though not its members) must subscribe to a statement of faith, or because it refused to accept among its officers those who advocated or practiced homosexuality."[7]

- The *Baehr v. Lewin* case before the Hawaii Supreme Court "ruled under the equal protection guarantee of the state constitution that Hawaii's statute restricting marriage to the union of a man and woman 'is presumed to be unconstitutional.'"[8]

- The Boy Scouts of America have been under attack for (a) not admitting girls; (b) not admitting atheists, and (c) not permitting avowed homosexuals to serve in any leadership capacity. The 2000 Supreme Court *Dale* decision ruled that the organization was a private organization and were entitled to choose their own members. The ACLU and others have pounced on the Scouts in numerous struggles, not about homosexuality, but forbidding a religious organization to use public land.[9]

- Catholic Charities in Massachusetts in 2010 was told that it "had to withdraw from its adoption service or change its policies and become willing to place children with same-sex couples."[10] "In 2008, the Supreme Court of California ruled that two physicians could

[4] Josh McDowell and Bob Hostetler, *The New Tolerance*, 45. Cited from "California Cross Lamp Must Be Kept under a Bushel," *World*, 20 [Sept. 1997], 19. The cross had been erected in 1934 and dedicated by Franklin D. Roosevelt. For years, it was a magnet for Easter sunrise and prayer services. "In a carefully crafted plan to save the cross, city supervisors in July voted unanimously to sell at auction the one-third of an acre of the park on which the cross stands to an Armenian American federation for $26,000. The group pledged to maintain the cross and grounds. It also agreed to stipulations by the lawsuit's plaintiffs. Among them: The cross no longer can be illuminated except twice a year, although ground lighting will be allowed year-round for safety purposes" (available online at *http://www.worldmag.com/1997/09/religion_notes/page3*, accessed March 15, 2014).

[5] The May 5, 1995 court papers read, "And make no mistake, the court is going to have a United States marshal in attendance at the graduation. If any student offends this court, that student will be summarily arrested and will face up to six months incarceration in the Galveston County Jail for contempt of court" [McDowell and Hostetler, 53; cited from Brannon Howse, "The People and Agenda of Multicultural Education, *Understanding the Times* (January 1997), p. 3].

[6] Robert H. Bork, *Slouching Toward Gomorrah*, 102.

[7] D. A. Carson, *The Intolerance of Tolerance*, 30.

[8] Bork, *op. cit.*, 112.

[9] Carson, *op. cit.*, 37.

[10] Carson, 38.

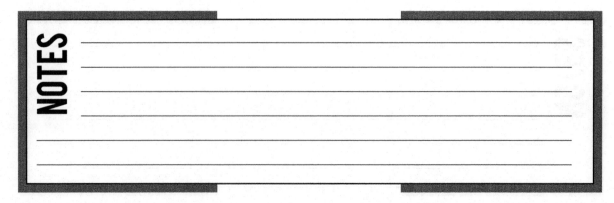

NOTES

not legally refuse artificial insemination to a woman because she was a lesbian."[11]

- Elane Photography, a business operated by a husband-wife Evangelical team, refused to photograph the gay commitment ceremony of two women. In 2006 Vanessa Willcock filed a complaint with the New Mexico Human Rights Commission, which eventually found against Elane Photography and ordered it to pay $6,637 for Willcock's legal fees. The decision was appealed to the District Court where again Elane Photography lost (December 2009).[12]

These incidents portend ominous days ahead for people faithfully adhering to the word of God. Are these indications that exclusion from the market place, the ability to earn a living, will come to those opposed to homosexuality? What about one's beliefs about abortion, euthanasia, unwed couples who live together, etc.?

Living in a Pagan Society

The world in which God's people live has never been God-fearing or Christian. Its morés, values, goals, etc. have always been different from those of the Lord. Even when we think back to the days of our youth when Christians values were more widely accepted than today, we remember that issues confronted God's people in our society. Should the county be "wet" or "dry"? (That is, should the county allow alcohol to be sold?) Should Christians attend the prom and other school sponsored dances. Fornication was prevalent, but mostly hidden. Drinking alcoholic beverages was common among teenagers. Immodest dress was an issue then (remember the mini-skirts?) even as it is today. Communities had public swimming pools where bikini-clad women were on display.

We should not think it strange that our world in twenty-first century America has different values than Christ. Christians are pilgrims and sojourners in every age in which they have lived (1 Chron. 29:15; Psa. 39:12; Heb. 11:13; 1 Pet. 1:17; 2:11).

New Testament instruction teaches one how to be submissive to a pagan, immoral, corrupt government. The wickedness of the Roman government was as bad as our own. Nevertheless, God's people were taught to be submissive to that government (Rom. 13:1-7; Tit. 3:1; 1 Pet. 2:13). Even pagan governments serve the purpose of keeping order in the land (Rom. 13:4). Even though governments spend funds on things that are morally sinful, we still must pay the taxes imposed on us (Rom. 13:6). Jesus said, "Render therefore to Caesar the things that are Caesar's, and to God the things that are God's" (Matt. 22:21; cf. 17:25). Christians have been instructed to pray for their rulers, especially to pray that they may be permitted to lead a quiet and peaceable life (1 Tim. 2:1-2). Christians can and have used available government protections to defend themselves from unwarranted suffering (Acts 16:25-40; 25:10-12). But should the day come when Christians are not permitted to live a quiet and peaceable life, they must resolve to obey God rather than men (Acts 4:19; 5:29).

Sometimes God's people have faced terrible ordeals from the hand of wicked governments. Pharaoh ordered that the male infants born to

---

[11] Carson, 39.

[12] Carson, 39. For additional information, see Thomas M. Messner, "New Mexico Photography Business Seeks Supreme Court Review," *http://www.heritage.org/research/reports/2014/01/new-mexico-photography-business-seeks-supreme-court-review*, accessed March 15, 2014.

NOTES
_____
_____
_____
_____
_____
_____

Israelite women be thrown into the river (Exod. 1:22). Daniel was thrown into the lions' den for praying in public (Dan. 6); the three Hebrew children, Shadrach, Meshach, and Abednego, were thrown into a fiery furnace because they refused to bow to the king's image (Dan. 3). Remember the ancient worthies:

> And what more shall I say? For the time would fail me to tell of Gideon and Barak and Samson and Jephthah, also of David and Samuel and the prophets: who through faith subdued kingdoms, worked righteousness, obtained promises, stopped the mouths of lions, quenched the violence of fire, escaped the edge of the sword, out of weakness were made strong, became valiant in battle, turned to flight the armies of the aliens. Women received their dead raised to life again. And others were tortured, not accepting deliverance, that they might obtain a better resurrection. Still others had trial of mockings and scourgings, yes, and of chains and imprisonment. They were stoned, they were sawn in two, were tempted, were slain with the sword. They wandered about in sheepskins and goatskins, being destitute, afflicted, tormented – of whom the world was not worthy. They wandered in deserts and mountains, in dens and caves of the earth. And all these, having obtained a good testimony through faith, did not receive the promise, God having provided something better for us, that they should not be made perfect apart from us (Heb. 11:32-40).

Should Christians face their own Holocaust in the days that lie ahead, we must learn to suffer for doing good, as did the Christians before us. They rejoiced that they were counted worthy to suffer for Christ (Acts 5:40-41; cf. 1 Pet. 1:6-9). Peter exhorted,

> Beloved, do not think it strange concerning the fiery trial which is to try you, as though some strange thing happened to you; but rejoice to the extent that you partake of Christ's sufferings, that when His glory is revealed, you may also be glad with exceeding joy. If you are reproached for the name of Christ, blessed are you, for the Spirit of glory and of God rests upon you. On their part He is blasphemed, but on your part He is glorified. But let none of you suffer as a murderer, a thief, an evildoer, or as a busybody in other people's matters. Yet if anyone suffers as a Christian, let him not be ashamed, but let him glorify God in this matter. For the time has come for judgment to begin at the house of God; and if it begins with us first, what will be the end of those who do not obey the gospel of God? Now "If the righteous one is scarcely saved, Where will the ungodly and the sinner appear?" Therefore let those who suffer according to the will of God commit their souls to Him in doing good, as to a faithful Creator (1 Pet. 4:12-19).

The book of Revelation pictures Satan using government to assault God's people (Rev. 13); it has happened before and it could happen again.

Can Christians Participate in Government?

Some brethren admonish Christians not to be involved in government. Some have taught that one is guilty of sin should he participate as a soldier in the military or as a police officer, because each is sometimes called upon to take someone's life. However, we see that Christians did participate in different roles of government. Cornelius was a soldier in the Roman army (Acts 10:1-2); both Matthew and Zacchaeus were tax collectors (Matt. 10:3; Luke 19:2); there were saints among Caesar's praetorian guard (Phil. 1:13, see RSV) and in his household (Phil. 4:22); Erastus served the city government at Corinth as the treasurer of the city (Rom. 16:23, NKJV); the Ethiopian eunuch was Queen Candace's treasurer (Acts 8:27); Joseph was second in command in Egypt (Gen. 41:40); Sheshbazzar

NOTES _____
_____
_____
_____
_____

was governor of Judah under Cyrus (Ezra 5:14) and Nehemiah was governor of the Persian province of Judah under Artaxerxes (Neh. 5:14); Saul, David, and Solomon served as kings; Joshua was head of the military; etc. The list could be extended.

Let us move this a step further. Solomon wrote, "When the righteous are in authority, the people rejoice; But when a wicked man rules, the people groan" (Prov. 29:2; see also vv. 8, 14; 25:4-5). These texts show how righteous men in positions of authority are a blessing to a land (cf. Prov. 16:12; 20:8; 29:14).

The fact is that God does not have one law for His people and another law for those who have not chosen to obey His word. He has *one* law which applies to all of mankind (Acts 17:30-31). If it is sinful for Christians to serve in the military or policemen, it is sinful for everyone to serve in those jobs. Christian should consider their situation fortunate when God-fearing men who exalt righteousness and punish wickedness are in control of government (Prov. 14:34).

We are fortunate to live in a country that encourages its citizens to participate in government and at all levels. Our ability to serve in such capacities is an opportunity to allow our righteous influence to affect the society in which we live (Matt. 5:13-16). Whereas the church has no divine authority to be involved in politics, individual Christians can serve in the political process, as one chooses to do so. Perhaps we have not done as much as we could to influence our nation for righteousness!

Conclusion

This lesson showed various relationships that God's people have had with government from approximately 2000 B.C. to A.D. 100. We are reminded that governments are constantly changing, and sometimes their attitude toward God's people changes rapidly from that of favored people to victims of persecution. Recognizing that this can occur, we examined the Scriptures that govern how Christians should react toward government and the attitudes necessary to survive hostile treatment at government's hand. United States Christians have been blessed to be able to participate in government and are blessed when righteous men occupy powerful positions in government, to influence government to righteousness.

Questions

1. What can one learn about a government's attitude toward God's people from Exodus 1? _____

   _____

2. Why do governments act with hostility toward religion? _____

   _____

3. What difference can you see between what happened in Exodus 1 and in Acts 16:16-40, when Paul and Silas were beaten and thrown into prison? _____

   _____

4. How do the following Scriptures define the Christian's attitude under systematic government hostility and under sporadic attacks?

   a. Acts 4:19-20 _____

   b. Matt. 22:37 _____

   c. Matt. 22:21 _____

   d. Phil. 3:20_____

5. What was government's attitude toward God's people in the days of ...

    a. Joseph? _____

    b. King Cyrus? _____

    c. King David? _____

6. For what does 1 Timothy 2:2 teach Christians to pray? _____

_____

7. Name four rulers in the Bible who could be identified as people of God. _____

_____

8. Give two examples when God-fearing rulers had difficulty in administering government. _____

_____

9. Why should Christians be wary of government and its tentacles? _____

_____

10. From your own observations (not those cited in the book), what are some ominous signs that the United States government could oppress God's people?_____

_____

11. What do the Scriptures mean when it uses "pilgrims" and "sojourners" to describe Christians (1 Chron. 29:15; Psa. 39:12; Heb. 11:13; 1 Pet. 1:17; 2:11)? _____

_____

12. What principles do the following passages teach about a Christian's relationship to government?

    a. Rom. 13:1; Tit. 3:1; 1 Pet. 2:13_____

    b. Rom. 13:4_____

    c. Rom. 13:6_____

    d. Acts 16:25-40 _____

    e. Heb. 11:32-40_____

    f. 1 Pet. 4:12-19_____

13. What role did each of the following play in government?

    a. Cornelius (Acts 10:1-2)?_____

    b. Matthew and Zacchaeus (Matt. 10:3; Luke 19:2)? _____

    c. Erastus (Rom. 16:23)? _____

    d. Ethiopian eunuch (Acts 8:27)? _____

    e. Joseph (Gen. 41:40)?_____

    f. Joshua? _____

    g. David? _____

14. What do these verses teach about righteous people administering government: Proverbs 16:12; 20:8; 29:2, 8, 14; 25:4-5; 29:14?_____

_____

The Education of Children

A quotation that is attributed to Francis Xavier (1506-1552) says, "Give me the children until they are seven, and anyone may have them afterwards." The idea is that they will be so well indoctrinated in Catholic thinking by age seven that the child will die a Catholic. Whether or not this is completely true, no one denies the power of the early influences on a child's adult life. If we recognize the influence of Catholic education on children, how much more should we be concerned about the influence of our public schools?

As the welfare state of the United States government expands, many parental obligations are being filled by government (providing health care, subsidizing rent, issuing food stamps, providing medical care, providing free cell phones, as well as education). The educational system has the children 6-8 hours every day for about 180 days a year. During those days, the schools feed some of the children three meals a day, and some schools also provide meals in the summer. Sometimes schools have to bathe the children, give them clean clothing, provide shoes, etc., to children whose parents are failing in these areas. This places an inordinate burden on teachers who are spending excessive amounts of time doing jobs that are parental responsibilities.

In many respects the schools are filling the role of parents.

Secular Humanism in the Schools

The American school system has been under the control of secular humanists for nearly 100 years. John Dewey (1859-1952) was an American philosopher whose ideas have been very influential in education; he was a major voice of progressive education[1] and liberalism. Dewey believed that the schools are a tool to "reconstruct society." He wrote,

> I believe that *education is the fundamental method of social progress and reform...* .

> I believe that the community's duty to education is, therefore, its paramount moral duty. By law and punishment, by social agitation and discussion, society can regulate and form itself in a more or less haphazard and chance way. But *through education society can formulate its own purposes*, can organize its own means and resources, and thus shape itself with

---

[1] For more information about progressive education, see *http://en.wikipedia.org/wiki/Progressive_education*, accessed 3/28/2014. Dewey's pragmatism was placed above moral absolutes and helped give rise to situational ethics.

Before and After	
What is your reaction to this attitude?	
I am responsible to be sure my children go to school and do their homework. It is the school's responsibility to teach them.	
Before	**After**

definiteness and economy in the direction in which it wishes to move. ...

I believe it is the business of every one interested in education to insist upon *the school as the primary and most effective instrument of social progress and reform in order that society may be awakened to realize what the school stands for*, and aroused to the necessity of endowing the educator with sufficient equipment properly to perform his task.[2]

One should note that Dewey's attitude was not that schools should teach math, science, history, etc., but that schools are a primary instrument to reform society in keeping with the goals and aspirations defined by his philosophical and religious beliefs. Significantly, John Dewey was one of the signatories of *Humanist Manifesto I*.[3] In *A Common Faith*, Dewey wrote that religion is not governed by some divinely inspired document.

Some fixed doctrinal apparatus is necessary for a religion. But faith in the possibilities of continued and rigorous inquiry does not limit access to truth to any channel or scheme of things. It does not say that truth is universal and then add there is but one road to it. It does not depend for assurance upon subjection to any dogma or item of dogma. It trusts that the natural interactions between man and his environment will breed more intelligence and generate more knowledge provided the scientific methods that define intelligence in operation are pushed further into the mysteries of the world, being themselves promoted and improved in

the operation. There is such a thing as faith in intelligence becoming religious in quality. ...

A body of beliefs and practices that are apart from the common and natural relations of mankind must, in the degree in which it is influential, weaken and sap the force of the possibilities inherent in such relations. Here lies one aspect of the emancipation of the religious from religion.[4]

So, the public classrooms are being used as the principle agency in the United States for emancipating the religious from their religion and spreading secular humanist values.[5]

How Secularism Affects the Schools

Charles Francis Potter, founder and leader of The First Humanist Society of New York, said, "Humanizing education consists largely of detheizing it."[6] He continued to explain the success humanists were having in education saying,

We have undergone a revolution in education since that day (the day when teachers used the Bible in education, mw), but the humanization of education is not yet complete.

We have eliminated to a large extent, except in certain denominational and parochial schools

---

[2] John Dewey, "My Pedagogic Creed," *School Journal* 54 (January 1897), 77-80. Available online at *http://dewey.pragmatism.org/creed.htm*, accessed 3/28/2014.

[3] *http://americanhumanist.org/Humanism/Humanist_Manifesto_I*.

[4] John Dewey, *A Common Faith,* 24-25.

[5] See Herbert Schlossberg, *Idols for Destruction*, 275.

[6] Potter, *Humanizing Religion*, 32. Potter is also quoted as having written in 1930, in his book *Humanism: A New Religion*, "Education is thus a most powerful ally of humanism, and every American school is a school of humanism. What can a theistic Sunday school's meeting for an hour once a week and teaching only a fraction of the children do to stem the tide of the five-day program of humanistic teaching?" (*http://www.secular-humanism.com/*, accessed 3/31/2014).

NOTES

the theistic content of teaching, but the theistic method still obtains to a deplorable degree.[7]

John Dewey's belief that the schools should be a government agency to reshape society has been echoed by others. John Dunphy wrote about the use of the educational system to propagate humanist principles as follows:

Expanding upon the role the public education establishment should play to bring about the goals described in the *Humanist Manifesto II*, John Dunphy wrote: "I am convinced that the battle for humankind's future must be waged and won in the public school classroom by teachers that correctly perceive their role as proselytizers of a new faith: a religion of humanity that recognizes and respects the spark of what theologians call divinity in every human being....[8]The classroom must and will become an arena of conflict between the old and new – the rotting corpse of Christianity, together with all its adjacent evils and misery, and the new faith of humanism, resplendent with the promise of a world in which the never-realized Christian ideal of 'love thy neighbor' will finally be achieved."[9]

Areas of Concern

1. Evolution. Humanists recognize that one of the main tools for propagating the principles of

---

[7] *Ibid.*, 37. The Secular Humanism web site commented on the success of these educators saying, "They have been absolutely successful in teaching children that God is imaginary and contrary to 'science'" (*http://www.secular-humanism.com/*, accessed 3/31/2014).

[8] Part of what is omitted from the Dunphy quote is this: "These teachers must embody the same selfless dedication as the most rabid fundamentalist preachers, for they will be ministers of another sort, utilizing a classroom instead of a pulpit to convey humanist values in whatever subject they teach, regardless of the educational level."

[9] *http://en.wikipedia.org/wiki/Humanist_Manifesto*, accessed 3/31/2014. The quotation also appears in "Humanism and the Public Schools," *Truth Magazine* XXVIII: 13 (July 5, 1984), 396-397, 410-411. It originally appeared in *The Humanist Magazine* (Jan./Feb., 1983, p. 6).

The TV As An Education Tool

In *A Secular Humanist Declaration*, Paul Kurtz wrote about the need to use TV media to transform America. He said,

In totalitarian societies, the media serve as the vehicle of propaganda and indoctrination. In democratic societies television, radio, films, and mass publishing too often cater to the lowest common denominator and have become banal wastelands. There is a pressing need to elevate standards of taste and appreciation. Of special concern to secularists is the fact that the media (particularly in the United States) are inordinately dominated by a pro religious bias. The views of preachers, faith healers, and religious hucksters go largely unchallenged, and the secular outlook is not given an opportunity for a fair hearing. We believe that television directors and producers have an obligation to redress the balance and revise their programming. Indeed, there is a broader task that all those who believe in democratic secular humanist values will recognize, namely, the need to embark upon a long term program of public education and enlightenment concerning the relevance of the secular outlook to the human condition (22-23).

Parents need to be aware of how the TV is being used to teach secular humanist values. What do TV shows teach us about the Bible, Jesus, miracles, and creation? About religious leaders? About pre-marital sex, extra-marital sex, homosexuality, polygamy? About foul language?

How aware are we of the teaching that is being done through the media of TV and movies? How well are we responding to that teaching as parents teaching our children and as gospel preachers answering the doctrines taught in our society?

secular humanism is the teaching of evolution.[10]

_____

[10] In an amazingly candid comment under the heading "Secular Humanism – Main Tool is Evolutionary Thought," *http://www.secular-humanism.com/* (accessed 3/31/2014) the author writes:

> To satisfy the fundamental question of "Where did we come from?" children are taught the doctrine of Evolution. The first plank of the *Humanist Manifesto* states: "Religious humanists regard the universe as self-existing and not created." The second plank states: "Humanism believes that man is a part of nature and that he has emerged as a result of a continuous process." Certainly, the public school system propagates the Humanist doctrine (clearly an atheistic "religion"), and thus, condemns the concept of God. This is an amazing irony. Creation Science has been successfully kept out of the public schools by organizations such as the American Civil Liberties Union (A.C.L.U.) on the grounds that Creation is religious, and the government should not support religion in any fashion. "In fact, evolution became in a sense a scientific religion; almost all scientists have accepted it, and many are prepared to 'bend' their observations to fit with it" (H. S. Lipson, FRS, Professor of Physics, University of Manchester, UK, "A Physicist Looks at Evolution," *Physics Bulletin*, vol. 31, May 1980, pg. 138).

> Yet Evolution has not been proved. Sir Arthur Keith, a famous British evolutionary anthropologist and anatomist, confesses, "Evolution is unproved and unprovable. We believe it only because the only alternative is special creation, and that is unthinkable." In fact, it seems that the Theory of Evolution is contrary to established science. George Wald, another prominent Evolutionist (a Harvard University biochemist and Nobel Laureate), wrote, "When it comes to the Origin of Life there are only two possibilities: creation or spontaneous generation. There is no third way. Spontaneous generation was disproved one hundred years ago, but that leads us to only one other conclusion,

Darwinian evolution has a death-grip on all other explanations for the origin of the universe and of mankind. The fact is undeniable that any account that affirms intelligent design and a Creator is excluded from school curricula and teachers can lose their jobs for teaching creation.[11] Paul Kurtz wrote in *A Secular Humanist Declaration,*

> ...the evolution of the species is supported so strongly by the weight of evidence that it is difficult to reject it. Accordingly, we deplore the efforts by fundamentalists (especially in the United States) to invade the science classrooms, requiring that creationist theory be taught to students and requiring that it be included in biology textbooks. This is a serious threat both to academic freedom and to the integrity of the educational process.[12]

The teaching of evolutionary theory is pervasive. Children are taught about dinosaurs living on the earth for 160 million years whereas humans have only been on earth 4-5 million years; "The Dinosaurs in History" material (age ranges 5 to 11) shows the changes in life over the past 543 million years.[13] The Biblical account is subtly being attacked even in pre-school

_____

that of supernatural creation. We cannot accept that on philosophical grounds; therefore, we choose to believe the impossible: that life arose spontaneously by chance!" ("The Origin of Life," *Scientific American*, 191:48, May 1954).

[11] For a list of "Ten Major Court Cases about Evolution and Creationism," see *http://ncse.com/taking-action/ten-major-court-cases-evolution-creationism*, accessed 3/28/2014.

[12] Paul Kurtz, *A Secular Humanist Declaration*, 21. Signed by 58 "leaders of thought."

[13] Taken from "Dinosaur 'Did You Know?' Cards" (age range 5 to 11), *http://www.teachingideas.co.uk/themes/dinosaurs/*, accessed 3/28/2014. I suggest that you do an internet search to see how pervasively evolutionary theory is taught in materials on dinosaurs.

NOTES

_____

_____

_____

_____

_____

_____

classes by teaching the old earth theory as part of the evolutionary theory.[14] The atheistic evolution theory attacks the faith of our children by: (a) denying the existence of God;[15] (b) denying supernatural events (miracles) and divine revelation; (c) asserting that man is only a more highly developed animal;[16] (d) asserting that morals are relative and autonomous. The theistic evolutionist attacks the faith of our children by denying what the Biblical record says about creation and the age of the earth, thus undermining confidence in divine revelation. Furthermore, should the child's parents challenge the school's teaching on evolution, they are frequently portrayed as uninformed, uneducated, and misguided by religious myths.

2. Attacks morality. The secularist position on ethics is called "situational ethics," "relativity in morals," "values clarification," or some other name. *A Secular Humanist Declaration* wrote this about "moral education":

---

[14] The reason for excluding religion from public schools is to protect defenseless children from religious indoctrination by forcing them to hear the Bible read or prayer being said in schools operated by the State. However, the State has force fed evolutionary dogma to our defenseless children for decades.

[15] The first affirmation of *Humanist Manifesto I* is this: "First: Religious humanists regard the universe as self-existing and not created."

[16] One may legitimately ask by what objective point of view one can declare that man is more highly developed than other animals. Is there a measuring stick to determine which is more highly evolved or is man egotistically elevating his own position? The cockroach, which has been on this earth 40-50 million years according to evolutionary theory, is able to survive in many diverse environment. How does one know that the cockroach is not more highly evolved than man? What is the measuring stick?

We believe that moral development should be cultivated in children and young adults. We do not believe that any particular sect can claim important values as their exclusive property; hence it is the duty of public education to deal with these values. Accordingly, we support moral education in the schools that is designed to develop an appreciation for moral virtues, intelligence, and the building of character. We wish to encourage wherever possible the growth of moral awareness and the capacity of free choice and an understanding of the consequences thereof. We do not think it is moral to baptize infants, to confirm adolescents, or to impose a religious creed on young people before they are able to consent. Although children should learn about the history of religious moral practices, these young minds should not be indoctrinated in a faith before they are mature enough to evaluate the merits for themselves. It should be noted that secular humanism is not so much a specific morality as it is a method for the explanation and discovery of rational moral principles.

Notice that the schools see their task as teaching moral values to our children – moral values that are not based on Christ's teaching but on secular humanist values.

Secular humanists do not believe that there are any moral absolutes. Everyone has his own value system and what is right for one person may not be right for another. However, no one has the right to be judgmental of another's values; of this secular humanists are absolutely positive – except humanists reserve the right to condemn the value system of Bible believers!

In the 1960s Sex Education in the Public Schools made its debut. The justification for the movement was to prevent venereal diseases, premarital pregnancy, etc. However, the program was not merely to present the biological facts about sex, but also to discuss

NOTES

_____
_____
_____
_____
_____
_____
_____

such moral issues as contraception, abortion, premarital and extramarital sex, homosexuality, masturbation, pornography, etc. – all from the secular humanist value system. Sex education is required in many states, although some allow parents to opt-out their children from the program. Whatever positive things can be said about sex education in the public schools, one thing is undeniable: the schools do not and cannot send out the message that sex outside of wedlock, homosexuality, and pornography are sinful or wrong. Indeed, humanism denies that morals need any theological sanctioning.[17] Many parents see the public education system as undermining their own teaching about sexual purity, condescendingly describing what Christian parents teach as puritanical and inhibiting. The school system has played an important role in undermining Christian values relating to fornication, adultery, and homosexuality.

Values Clarification has been used in schools to reshape the child's values. The program, developed by humanist psychologists Abraham Maslow and Carl Rogers, is well-known for its description of a given situation and then forcing the participants to make hard choices about what should be done in that given situation. For example, ten people are stranded in a lifeboat with enough supplies for eight people to survive ten days with the strictest rationing. Making it back to land will take ten days, so what should be done? The ten people in the lifeboat include one with Down syndrome and a 90 year-old-man who is barely able to move. The group then is faced with the situation of having to determine what to do. The obvious implication is that the one with

Down syndrome and the aged person should be thrown overboard so that the other eight can survive. This "values clarification" exercise is used to teach situational ethics – the ability to make one's own decision independent of Biblical instruction and based on the situations one faces. Using Values Clarification, any moral absolute can be eliminated because every form of conduct is permissible "given the situation." The result of values clarification is to undermine confidence in moral absolutes, opening the children to be accepting of things they may have been taught at home to be sinful/wrong, such as fornication, homosexuality, abortion, etc.

3. Attacks religion. The secular viewpoint of religion is clearly defined in its literature. In 1933, *Humanist Manifesto I* saw humanism itself as a more highly evolved and rational religion than Christianity. According to *Humanist Manifesto II* (1973) "humanists still believe that traditional theism, especially faith in the prayer-hearing God, assumed to live and care for persons, to hear and understand their prayers, and to be able to do something about them, is an unproved and outmoded faith." "We find insufficient evidence for belief in the existence of a supernatural; it is either meaningless or irrelevant to the question of survival and fulfillment of the human race. As nontheists, we begin with humans not God, nature not deity." In *A Secular Humanist Declaration*, humanists "find insufficient evidence for the claim that some divine purpose exists for the universe. They reject the idea that God has intervened miraculously in history or revealed himself to a chosen few, or that he can save or redeem sinners. ... We reject the divinity of Jesus, the divine mission of Moses... . We do not accept as true the literal interpretation of the Old and New Testaments."[18] Given these

---

[17] *A Secular Humanist Declaration* says that "ethical judgments can be formulated independently of revealed religion" saying, "We are opposed to Absolutist morality" (pp. 14-15).

[18] *Ibid.*, 18.

NOTES _____
_____
_____
_____
_____
_____
_____

When Do Our Children Quit Going to Church?

Of those thousand 20 to 29-year-old evangelicals who attended church regularly but no longer do so:

- 95% of them attended church regularly during their elementary and middle school years

- 55% attended church regularly during high school

- 11% were still going to church during their early college years (Ken Ham and Britt Beemer, *Already Gone*, 31).

presuppositions, how would one expect religion to be treated in our public schools?

I have a B.A. in religious studies from Butler University, a M.A. in religious studies from Christian Theological Seminary and a M.A. in religious studies from Indiana University. Therefore, I have some perception about how religion is taught in both public and private education. The commonly taught religious studies class on world religion is to teach that all religions are equally valid expressions of man's efforts to worship a divine being. World religions studies view the variety of world religions, including both Judaism and Christianity, as Paul viewed the pagan religions at Athens: "that they should seek the Lord, in the hope that they might grope for Him and find Him, though He is not far from each one of us" (Acts 17:27). Religion is seen as man's creation. Usually it explained as man's attempt to understand nature – the change of seasons, the power of the sun, thunder, and other natural powers that have been objects of worship. Worship then was thought to have evolved through various stages: animism, polytheism, henotheism, monotheism, Christianity. Post-modernism attacks the modernist's model saying there is no evidence to support the evolutionary development of religion (in books explaining the evolutionary development of religion, modern religions in third world countries were used to explain ancient religious thought; there is no sequence of historical evidences to trace the evolutionary development of religion). Also, modernism assumed the superiority of Christianity. Based on its premise that there is no absolute truth, post-modernism teaches that all religious are be equally valid and none is superior to the others. Since all religions are equally valid, preaching Christianity to another world is seen as an arrogant presumption that Western religion is superior to any other religion. What God described as a virtue – to take the gospel into all the world (Matt. 28:18-20; Mark 16:15-16) – is now seen as a vice!

The Failing Schools

Many of the public schools are in serious trouble, especially the inner-city schools. American children are not competing as well against those educated in other countries as they once did.[19] There is not one cause of these failures; certainly we need to acknowledge the hard work that conscientious teachers are doing, many of whom are being compelled by the

---

[19] Students in the United States performed near the middle of the pack. On average 16 other industrialized countries scored above the United States in science, and 23 scored above us in math (*http://www.greatschools.org/students/academic-skills/1075-u-s-students-compare.gs*, accessed 3/31/2014). I suggest that you do some research to see how your own school is performing.

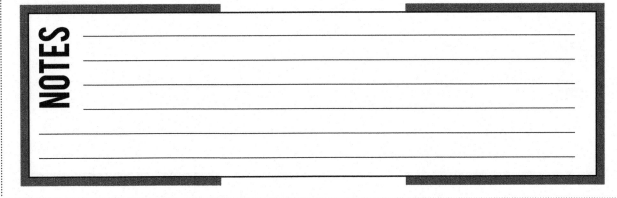

NOTES

educational system to do things that they think are counter-productive or wrong-headed. Having acknowledged this, let us note these things.

When Do Our Children Become Unbelievers?

Those who no longer believe that all of the accounts and stories in the Bible are true:

- 39.8% first had doubts in middle school

- 43.7% first had their doubts in high school

- 10.6 had their first doubts during college (Ken Ham and Britt Beemer, *Already Gone*, 33).

The Faith of our Children is Already Being Undermined in Middle School!

Inner city schools are failing because of the broken families. Mothers and daddies are not involved in the education of their children.

Concerned parents are taking their children out of the school systems. Some are moving them from inner-city schools to the suburbs; some are enrolling their children in private schools and others are home schooling. The result is that the salt is being removed from the school environment, leaving the rest in rapidly deteriorating condition.

What We Can Do

1. Accept responsibility for the education of your children. God has not given the United States Department of Education responsibility to rear your children; he has given that responsibility to parents. God holds parents responsible for training their children to be able to hold a job when they are adults, to know right from wrong, and to know about God (Deut. 6:4-9; see the book of Proverbs; Eph. 6:1-4). The parent who thinks he can take his children to school and trust the school to educate his children is misguided.

2. Be involved in your children's school. Be a volunteer at school. Get to know their teachers and principal. Read their textbooks enough to know what they are being exposed to.

3. Know their friends. Peer pressure is a very big influence on your children's lives. How well do you know their friends?

4. Read to your children and with your children. Reading is one of the basic building blocks of education. If your child is behind in reading skills by the third grade,[20] he rarely catches up.

5. Realize the educational and moral environment in which your children are placed and work to teach them God's word to overcome the influences of that environment. If Eunice and Lois could raise a God-fearing son in the first-century moral environment, Christians can raise God-fearing children in the twenty-first century (2

---

[20] "Results of a longitudinal study of nearly 4,000 students find that those who don't read proficiently by third grade are four times more likely to leave school without a diploma than proficient readers. For the worst readers, those who couldn't master even the basic skills by third grade, the rate is nearly six times greater. While these struggling readers account for about a third of the students, they represent more than three fifths of those who eventually drop out or fail to graduate on time" (Hernandez, *Double Jeopardy: How Third-Grade Reading Skills and Poverty Influence High School Graduation*, p. 3).

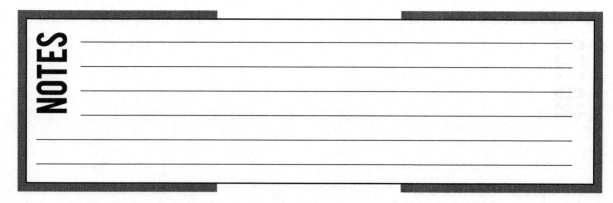

NOTES

Tim. 1:5; 3:14-17). Given the secular influences in the American school system, is it any wonder that Christians are losing so many of their children to the world?

6. Make their spiritual training more important than anything else. There will be scheduling conflicts in your child's life in which responsibilities to God conflict with school activities. This is an opportunity to teach your children Bible priorities – to seek first the kingdom of God and His righteousness (Matt. 6:33). Teach your children the proper priorities. There will be peer pressure to do things that God disapproves (immodest dress, dancing, the prom, etc.). Help your children to make the proper decisions. If they lack the moral fortitude to make the right decision, make it for them and work to make them strong enough to make the right decision next time (see Song of Sol. 8:8-9).

Conclusion

The public school system is being used to transmit the value system of secular humanism, pluralism, or atheism. Secularism is an evangelistic religion that is being spread throughout our culture through many sources, including the public education system. It is undermining our children's faith. We have witnessed children of God-fearing parents who walk away from God when they leave home. These children have adopted the values of the world and rejected the Christian faith. This lesson has been designed to make us aware of how the public school system is being used to spread atheistic values.

Questions

1. What did Francis Xavier mean when he said, "Give me the children until they are seven and anyone may have them afterwards"? _____

   _____

2. What parental roles are being filled by schools? _____

   _____

3. According to John Dewey, what is a primary goal of the educational system?_____

   _____

4. What was Dewey's belief about books claiming to be inspired revelations? _____

   _____

5. What did Charles Francis Potter mean when he said, "Humanizing education consists of *detheizing* it"?_____

   _____

NOTES
_____
_____
_____
_____
_____
_____

6. Explain John Dunphy's vision of the educational system. _____
_____

7. How does teaching children evolution lay the foundation for secularism or atheism? _____
_____

8. What do humanist/atheists teach about ethics? _____
_____

   a. Does the school trust parents teaching their own children about ethics?_____
_____

   b. What moral principles have the sex education classes at school taught? _____
_____

   c. What moral principles do values clarification activities teach? _____
_____

9. What beliefs underlie humanist teaching about religion? _____
_____

   a. How does Acts 17:27 describe man's religious efforts in the absence of divine revelation? ____
_____

   b. What is the evolutionary theory of religion? _____
_____

   c. How do post-modernists attack the evolutionary theory of religion?_____
_____

   d. What does humanism believe about Christian evangelism? _____
_____

10. What is your opinion of urban schools?_____
_____

11. Who is responsible for your child's education? _____
_____

NOTES
_____
_____
_____
_____
_____

The Family

That the family is under attack in American society is obvious. Significant changes that are occurring in the American family include the following:

- more gay and lesbian couples raising children
- more unmarried couples raising children
- more fatherless homes
- more people living together without getting married
- more mothers of young children working outside the home
- more women choosing not to have children

The purpose of this lesson is to examine what has been the influence of secularism in our society on the family unit. We will show how the family is being redefined to reflect secular values. We will look at a number of influences in our society that have attacked the home.

Public institutions (schools, hospitals, etc.) have to deal with people in all of these relationships. Their workers are trained to be inclusive in their approach to family. The Lesbian, Gay, Bisexual and Transgender Equal Rights (LGBT) group recommends this definition of family be used by hospitals to define "family" for visitation purposes:

"Family" means any person(s) who plays a significant role in an individual's life. This may include a person(s) not legally related to the individual. Members of "family" include spouses, domestic partners,[1] and both different-sex and same-sex significant others. "Family" includes a minor patient's parents, regardless of the gender of either parent. Solely for purposes of visitation policy, the concept of parenthood is to be liberally construed without limitation as encompassing legal parents, foster parents, same-sex parent, step-parents, those serving *in loco parentis*, and other persons operating in caretaker roles.[2]

This accommodation to the living arrangements of Americans reflects and coincides with the secular agenda for redefining family. The *aboundingjoy.com* website contrasted the beliefs between secular humanists and Christians in several areas, one of which was family. Here is what they described secular humanists to believe about family:

---

[1] The article makes this additional comment about "domestic partners": "It should also be noted that the term 'domestic partners' in this definition encompasses not only domestic partnerships but also all legally recognized same-sex relationships, including civil unions and reciprocal beneficiary arrangements."

[2] "LGBT-Inclusive Definitions of Family" for healthcare organizations (*http://www.hrc.org/resources/entry/lgbt-inclusive-definitions-of-family*, accessed 4/1/2014).

Before and After	
How do you react?	
Your child brings home a handout from school that features a family in which a child has two mothers – obviously living as a lesbian couple.	
Before	**After**

Secular Humanists prefer to think of "family" in larger groups of perhaps unrelated people. Many secular humanists would affirm the legitimacy of same-sex marriages or civil unions. Many would deny the importance of fathers, encouraging "single parenting by choice." Many secular humanists trust schools more than parents to know what is best for children. Some humanists believe that the child's first responsibility is to a representative of the state, not necessarily to the parents. (For example, humanists often support the right of a child to an abortion without parental consent.)[3]

The TV has redefined family in its programming.[4]

- Nuclear family (father, mother, kids): *Father Knows Best*
- Widowed family: *My Three Sons*
- Blended (widowed and possibly divorced and remarried) family: *The Brady Bunch*
- Racially mixed family: *The Jeffersons*
- Two singles living together with reversed roles: *Who's the Boss?*
- Community of singles: *Three's Company, Friends*
- Homosexual family: *Modern Family*
- Polygamous family: *Sister Wives*

I suspect most readers have been troubled by the concerted effort to make homosexuality an "alternative lifestyle" in America. The sad fact is that TV is doing an effective job of making homosexual behavior more acceptable in America. Meg James wrote for the Los Angeles *Times*:

> Broadcast networks have shown dramatic improvement in their depiction of gays, lesbians and transgender characters in prime-time programming in the last year, according to a new study.
>
> Gay rights organization GLAAD on Friday gave high marks to ABC Family, Fox Broadcasting,[5] ABC, NBC and CW for their inclusiveness and positive portrayal of gays, lesbians and transgender characters on television.
>
> The scores were given as part of GLAAD's 7th Annual Network Responsibility Index.[6]

Not only are lesbian, gay, and transgender people being presented in positive light, but also those who stand opposed to homosexual and transgender behavior are consistently vilified.

Same-Sex Marriage

Government is reacting to the popularization of same-sex marriage. In September 1996, in response to moves by the state of Hawaii to recognize homosexual marriages, the Congress of the United States passed "The Defense of Marriage Acts" (DOMA).

> §1738C. No State, territory, or possession of the United States, or Indian tribe, shall be required to give effect to any public act, record, or judicial proceeding of any other State, territory,

---

[3] *http://www.aboundingjoy.com/humanism_chart.htm*, accessed 3/31/2014.

[4] For a description of the evolution of the family on network TV, see pp. 16-18 in my chapter "Build Strong Homes," the introductory material to *Build Strong Homes*. This material looks at how the family has been presented on TV from *Father Knows Best* to *Modern Family* (1950-2013).

[5] Many Christians think that Fox Broadcasting is supportive of conservative values. Pay attention to what this gay/lesbian organization perceives about Fox Broadcasting and beware!

[6] Meg James, "GLAAD: TV Networks Improve in Portrayal of Gays and Lesbians," *http://www. latimes.com/entertainment/envelope/cotown/la-et-ct-glaad-television-study-20131010,0,2666042. story#axzz2xYvUecga*, accessed 3/31/2014.

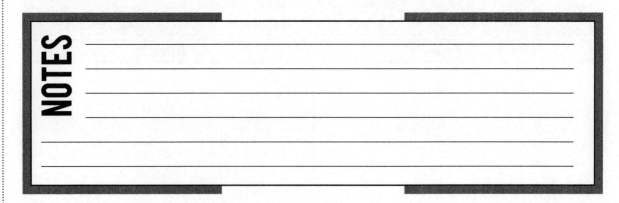

NOTES

_____
_____
_____
_____
_____
_____

possession, or tribe respecting a relationship between persons of the same sex that is treated as a marriage under the laws of such other State, territory, possession, or tribe, or a right or claim arising from such relationship.

DOMA defined "marriage" and "spouse" as follows:

In determining the meaning of any Act of Congress, or of any ruling, regulation, or interpretation of the various administrative bureaus and agencies of the United States, the word "marriage" means only a legal union between one man and one woman as husband and wife, and the word "spouse" refers only to a person of the opposite sex who is a husband or a wife.

At the time this is being written, seventeen states and the District of Columbia have legalized same-sex marriage.[7] Some states recognize homosexual marriages performed in other states, but not their own (Oregon, Ohio, Missouri, and Colorado). District courts have declared state constitutional amendments banning same-sex marriage unconstitutional under the Constitution of the United States in Utah, Oklahoma, Virginia, Texas, and Michigan. This information will soon be outdated, but the issue will not be gone. Though Christians have always had to live as pilgrims and sojourners in this world, as our society is increasingly dominated by atheistic humanism we are reminded of this truth more regularly.

---

[7] These states are California, Connecticut, Delaware, Hawaii, Illinois, Iowa, Maine, Maryland, Massachusetts, Minnesota, New Hampshire, New Jersey, New Mexico, New York, Rhode Island, Vermont, and Washington.

Earlier Assaults on the Family

As devastating as the homosexual assault on the family is, it has not been nearly so devastating as some earlier attacks. Think about how these movements have affected the family:

No-fault divorce.[8] The Lord Jesus taught that there is but one cause of divorce which allows the innocent party to remarry: fornication (Matt. 19:3-9). Throughout history, men and women have rebelled against God's teaching. In an earlier period in American history, divorce was difficult to obtain because one had to prove that his spouse's faults caused the divorce. Increasingly, men and women wanted to end their marriages whether or not the mate was at fault. California was the first U.S. State to adopt no-fault divorce in 1969.[9] Between 1960

---

[8] No-fault divorce is a divorce in which the dissolution of a marriage does not require a showing of wrong-doing by either party

[9] The article on "No-Fault Divorce" on *Wikipedia* says, "The earliest precedent in no-fault divorce laws was originally enacted in Russia shortly after the Bolshevik Revolution. They were legislated in the series of decrees that issued in early 1918. The decrees included nonjudicial dissolution of marriage by either party and mandatory provision of child-support. The purpose of the Soviet no-fault divorce laws was ideological, intended to revolutionize society at every level. They were the subject of significant revisional efforts from World War II to the 1960s. Major revisions were concluded in 1968. The Soviet 1968 and California 1969 no-fault divorce laws bore many detailed similarities of terminology, substance, and procedure" (accessed 4/1/2014). The article states that, according to Nikolai Krylenko, a chief architect of the Soviet law of marriage and leading theorist of "socialist legality" in the 1920s and 1930s, "the purpose of divorce without restraint was a step toward the ultimate goal of the abolition of marriage, thereby establishing the socialist transformation of society."

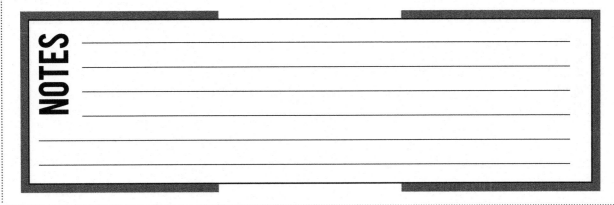

NOTES

and 1997, the divorce rate in America more than doubled.[10] Since 1996, the divorce rates leveled off and have begun to decrease. There are various reasons why the rate is decreasing (people waiting longer to get married, bad economy, high cost to get a divorce) but certainly one reason for the decrease in the divorce rate in recent years is that couples are living together outside of wedlock.

Cohabitation outside of wedlock. Sex outside the marriage bond is called "fornication" in the Bible and is revealed to be a work of the flesh that leads to eternal damnation (Gal. 5:19; 1 Cor. 6:12-20). Throughout human history, couples have been guilty of fornication. However, the sexual liberation movement of the 1960s rejected Christian values regarding sex; couples began to live together openly outside the bonds of marriage. The number of cohabiting couples increased from 439,000 in 1960 to 4.24 million in 1998 – an almost tenfold increase. During the 1990s, the number of cohabiting households increased by almost 50 percent.[11] Cohabitation was once taboo in America, but Hollywood Stars living together outside of wedlock encouraged others to follow their example. However, the homes of cohabiting couples are more unstable than are those of married couples. According to "Why More Parents Are Choosing Cohabitation Over Marriage," "The National Marriage Project report found two-thirds of kids will see their cohabitating parents break up by age 12, while only one-quarter of married-before-children parents will divorce. 'Cohabiting parents tend to be more ambivalent, which can lead to instability in the relationship,' says Margaret Owen, Ph.D., director of the Center for Children and Families at the University of Texas, Dallas. 'Perhaps this ambivalence is a factor in their decision to live together rather than get married in the first place.'"[12]

Redefining man's role in the home. The Bible defines the role of both husband and wife in the marriage relationship. It clearly states that the husband is the head of the home as Christ is the head of the church (Eph. 5:23-31). His role as head over the home is modeled after Christ's headship over the church – loving the church so much that He gave Himself for it, nourishing and cherishing the church. The Bible does not teach or approve tyrannical headship by the man over the home. The feminist movement views marriage as a patriarchal institution that benefits men and oppresses women. Women need to escape from the male dominance that exists in the family.[13] In vitro fertilization has given a woman the ability to conceive a child without a man being involved in her life. Radical feminists

---

Then follows the following paragraph quoted from "The Russian Effort to Abolish Marriage," *The Atlantic Monthly* (July, 1926), pp. 104-114:

Of course, if living together and not registration is taken as the test of a married state, polygamy and polyandry may exist; but the State can't put up any barriers against this. Free love is the ultimate aim of a socialist State; in that State marriage will be free from any kind of obligation, including economic, and will turn into an absolutely free union of two beings. Meanwhile, though our aim is the free union, we must recognize that marriage involves certain economic responsibilities, and that's why the law takes upon itself the defense of the weaker partner, from the economic standpoint.

[10] William J. Bennett, *The Index of Leading Cultural Indicators,* 68.

[11] *Ibid.,* 64, 65.

[12] *http://www.parenting.com/article/ cohabitation,* accessed 4/1/2014.

[13] Simone de Beauvoir, *The Second Sex*, 100.

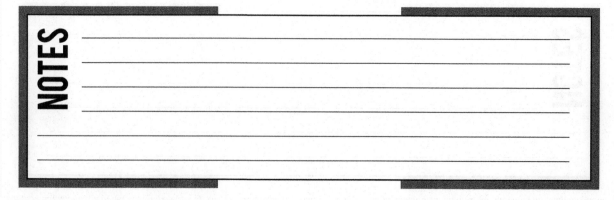

NOTES

have the attitude that a man is not needed in the lives of children.[14] Whether caused by feminist teaching, divorce, or ending cohabitation arrangements, the fact is that many children are being reared in fatherless homes.

- Between 1990 and 1998, the percentage of families that are headed by a single parent increased 13 percent. Between 1960 and 1998, the percentage of single-parent families more than tripled.[15]
- More than one-third (36 percent) of American children in 1990 were living apart from their biological fathers.[16]
- Nearly 80 percent of black women will be the head of the family at some point in their childbearing years.[17]

Indeed, the home in America has deteriorated in the last seventy-five years. As Christians, we need to be aware of what is happening among us and address what needs to be changed to improve the home.

Satan's Assault on the Family Is Not New

The changes we see in American culture with reference to family shock us. Perhaps it would be helpful for us to take a deep breath and regroup. We need to remember that Satan has aimed his arrows at the family throughout human history. Think about these perversions of family that we see in the Bible:

---

[14] Compare how TV has presented the father in such sitcoms as *Father Knows Best, All in the Family, and The Cosby Show.*

[15] Bennett, 57.

[16] *Ibid.*, 58.

[17] Bennett, *op. cit.*, 59.

- Polygamy (Gen. 4:19)
- Concubinage (Gen. 22:24; 35:22; 36:12; etc.)
- Serial monogamy by divorcing one's mate (Deut. 24:1-4; Matt. 19:3)
- Adultery (Lev. 20:10; Deut. 22:22)
- Sodomy (Gen. 19)
- Slavery broke up families (Gen. 37:36; 39:1; Exod. 21:1-11)

We should recognize that the times in which we live are not unique; God's people have lived in similar circumstances before.

God Defines and Joins in Marriage

As we witness what is happening around us, we should remind ourselves of some very basic, fundamental truths.

God created marriage for man's benefit. Marriage originated in the Garden of Eden. In God's wisdom, man was created first; only when he sensed his need for companionship did God create Eve to be a helper suited for man's needs (Gen. 2:18-24). Rather than viewing marriage as an institution that was created by man and evolved over the centuries, we need to remember that marriage between a man and woman is God's will and what is best for both man and woman. Furthermore, it is the environment God designed for bringing children into this world and rearing them.

God defines what marriage is. God is the one who determined that one man should be joined to one woman. Marriage is for heterosexuals. Despite what civil laws are passed in various state houses and in Washington, D.C., God has defined what constitutes marriage. Should *Sister Wives* open the door for general acceptance of polygamy and the LGBT group popularize

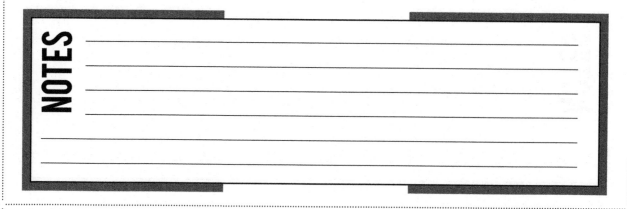

NOTES
_____
_____
_____
_____
_____
_____

homosexual marriages, the Scriptures will still define for mankind what marriage is. Man's deviation therefrom is evidence of his rebellious defiance of God's word, but does not change God's law.

God joins man and woman in marriage (Matt. 19:6; Prov. 2:17; Mal. 2:14). Only God can join two people in marriage and only God can separate them. Civil governments and churches may try to redefine marriage to include homosexual relationships, but only God can join two people in marriage. What is true with reference to homosexuality is also true with reference to divorce and remarriage. Human courts may join in marriage and issue legal decrees dissolving marriage, but these civil actions no more change what God has spoken than do pronouncements that homosexuals are married (or divorced).

Conclusion

Efforts to redefine what family is stem from a secular humanist agenda that is discontent with Christian values. Social changes within the United States, such as no-fault divorce, cohabitation outside of wedlock, redefining man's role in the home, and same-sex marriage, have deteriorated the home. Christians recognize that this is not the first time that Satan has tried to destroy the home and accept that their lives will be governed by God's word, regardless of what the American courts define "marriage" and "family" to be. Christians have had to do this for decades, as no-fault divorce ravaged homes and serial polygamy has become common in our country; Christians will allow their lives to be governed by God's word, regardless of what America decides about same-sex marriages.

Questions

1. What is meant by "family" according to ...

   a. Bible _____

   _____

   b. Modern America _____

   _____

2. How has TV reshaped the definition of "family"? _____

   _____

3. How has government responded to gay marriage? _____

   _____

4. What effect has "no-fault divorce" laws had on the family? ____

   _____

NOTES
_____
_____
_____
_____
_____

5. What does God teach about divorce and remarriage (Matt. 19:3-12)?_____
_____

6. How has cohabitation without marriage affected families?_____
_____
_____

7. What does the Bible say about cohabitation without marriage?_____
_____

8. What has contributed to fatherless homes? _____
_____

9. How was the husband portrayed in the following TV programs:
   a. Father Knows Best? _____
   _____
   _____

   b. All in the Family? _____
   _____
   _____

   c. The Cosby Show? _____
   _____
   _____

10. List six different departures from God's design for marriage that are mentioned in the Bible.
   a._____
   b._____
   c._____
   d._____
   e._____
   f. _____

NOTES _____
_____
_____
_____
_____
_____

11. How did marriage originate, according to ...

   a. The Bible?_____

   b. Atheism? _____

12. What is God's definition of marriage? _____

_____

13. Why is it important to understand that only God can join in marriage or loose one from a marriage? _____

_____

14. Why is this important? _____

_____

Moral Standards

It is easy for me to forget that a freshman in the 2015 college class was born in 1997. What I see as a major shift in public morality in our country is what he sees as the way it has always been. To him, the moral values in our society are normal; to me they are abhorrent violations of the moral principles revealed and taught by God. So, a brief recapitulation of the change in American society may be beneficial. For the older adults, this review will only briefly mention the events they have witnessed in their adult life; for the younger among us, perhaps it will give some background, not only for understanding their elders, but also as a measurement for the sickness in American society. The purpose of this chapter is to emphasize that the rejection of the Christian value system has created a culture of hedonism in America.

The Way It Was

I was about eight years old when my family got its first television. Prior to that, we listened to the radio for news and entertainment (radios used to broadcast programs such as *Roy Rogers and Dale Evans, The Lone Ranger*, etc.). When we got our television, we were able to pick up one channel and, after a few years and with a good antennae, we could watch two or three more channels. My generation watched such sit-coms as *I Love Lucy, Father Knows Best,*

and a host of serials in which the bad guys were always exposed for what they were (they were not sympathetically portrayed so that the viewing audience rooted for the bad guys). We identified with these shows because they so nearly resembled our own lives. We lived with both of our biological parents and they were involved in disciplining us. Society was much safer then. When we left home, we did not bother locking the doors; we closed the screens to keep out the flies. We were not afraid of thieves breaking into our houses. Men hung .30-.30 Rifles in the gun rack in the back of their pickups, parked them on Main Street with their windows down, did their shopping, and returned without concern for whether or not the rifles would be there when they returned. We did not have drive-by or school shootings.

Our way of life took a drastic turn in the 1960s when a cultural revolution that had been brewing for years broke out. Reaction during the Vietnam War was the occasion for civil disobedience, student frenzy, and an outbreak of violence; a rejection of traditional American values soon led to a social and cultural revolution that took many forms. Student riots burned down the ROTC buildings on campuses of numerous universities; at the same time racial unrest in America had people marching in the streets (the segregation of America needed to be changed). The Woodstock Festival

Before and After	
What do you think?	
To change America, Christians need to become actively involved in political action groups so that we can elect conservative state and federal officials.	
Before	**After**

(1969) was a music festival that was performed outdoors to an audience of hundreds of thousands; it was a definitive nexus for the countercultural movement that reveled in rock music, drugs, and sex. Homosexuals in Greenwich Village in NYC reacted to a police raid on June 27, 1969 by spontaneous, violent demonstrations. The gay community "came out of the closet" and began organizing eventually to become one of America's strongest lobby groups. Their first Gay Pride marches took place in 1970. The Sexual Revolution was characterized by a dramatic shift in traditional values related to sex, and sexuality. Sex outside the strict boundaries of heterosexual marriage became more socially acceptable. The feminist movement, which refers to a series of campaigns for reforms on issues such as reproductive rights (i.e., easy access to birth control, right to abortion on demand), domestic violence, maternity leave, equal pay, women's suffrage, sexual harassment, and sexual violence, attacked some legitimate inequalities in society that needed correction, but its defense of abortion, homosexuality, and attacks against the family obscured many of their legitimate complaints. These social forces created the political and religious left in our country.

On May 4, 1970, the Ohio National Guard tried to stop protesters on the campus of Kent State. Four were killed and nine others wounded. The effect of this was the quieting of protests on college campuses, but the young people who marched in the streets in the 1960s had not changed their minds. Robert H. Bork, who was nominated for the Supreme Court but was rejected by the liberal left that then controlled the Senate, wrote about this era:

> As the rioting and riotousness died down in the early 1970s and seemingly disappeared altogether in the last half of that decade and in the 1980s, it seemed, at last, that the Sixties were over. They were not. It was a malignant decade that, after a fifteen-year remission, returned in the 1980s to metastasize more devastatingly throughout our culture than it had in the Sixties, not with tumult but quietly, in the moral and political assumptions of those who now control and guide our major cultural institutions. The Sixties radicals are still with us, but now they do not paralyze the universities; they run the universities.[1]

But the liberals did not just go into universities; they went into politics, journalism, church bureaucracies, public institutions, etc. and propagated their opinions and wielded their influences. Bill Clinton (1946-   ) was the first president of the baby boomer generation (1946-1964). His election as president is evidence of how widely the liberalism of the 1960s had permeated American culture. Even his sordid affair with Monica Lewinsky was not enough to prevent his re-election for a second term.

What Happened to American Morals

Throughout the nineteenth and twentieth centuries, theological liberalism had attacked the Bible's historical accuracy[2] and doctrinal content.[3] In the 1960s, Biblical morality came under attack. Secular humanists who denied the existence of God devised a moral code independently of God. *Humanist Manifesto II* said, "We affirm that moral values derive their source from human

---

[1] Bork, *Slouching Toward Gomorrah*, 51.

[2] Liberalism denied that creation occurred in six days, choosing to believe instead in evolution (at first theistic and later atheistic). Biblical narratives that involved the miraculous were dismissed as myth and legend.

[3] The inspiration of Scripture, deity of Christ, resurrection of Jesus, and other important Biblical doctrines were denied.

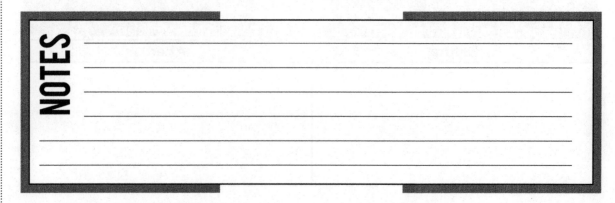

NOTES
_____
_____
_____
_____
_____
_____

experience. Ethics is autonomous and situational needing no theological or ideological sanction." In the area of sexual conduct, humanists deplored those efforts to "unduly repress sexual conduct." "The right to birth control, abortion, and divorce should be recognized. While we do not approve of exploitive, denigrating forms of sexual expression, neither do we wish to prohibit, by law or social sanction, sexual behavior between consenting adults. The many varieties of sexual exploration should not in themselves be considered 'evil'. ... individuals should be permitted to express their sexual proclivities and pursue their lifestyles as they desire."

The "clergy" joined the humanists in ethics.[4] Joseph Fletcher (1905-1991) was ordained as an Episcopal priest and taught ethics at Episcopal Divinity School and Harvard Divinity School. Later, he became an atheist, and signed *Humanist Manifesto II*. He published a book entitled *Situation Ethics* that argued for a new morality, "The new morality, situation ethics, declares that anything and everything is right or wrong, according to the situation."[5] *The new morality is absolutely positive that there are no absolutes!*

The new morality has had its corrosive effect in society. For a time, society seemed to be no worse from the teachings of situation ethics and humanist ethics. But the seed that was sown had not yet born its fruit. We are sixty years into the influence of humanist ethics. We can begin to see what kind of crop it has produced. Consider the following:

- Homosexuality led to the AIDS epidemic

- Sexual promiscuity leads to single-parent homes and abortion
- No-fault divorce has led to fatherless homes
- Fatherless homes have given rise to violent crime and a larger prison population
- American greed nearly brought down the economy through selling unsecured investments
- Drug crimes have made inner cities extremely violent
- Episodes of violence (Oklahoma City bombing, school shootings, etc.)
- The content of movies and TV programing show nudity, contain filthy language, exalt vengeance, etc.
- The lyrics of pop music are so raunchy that one cannot even quote them in a publication such as this[6]

Laura Ingraham cited this evidence of cultural rot: "preteen girls dressed as streetwalkers; disheveled boys wearing pants below their underwear; mothers in ultratight jeans and low-cut shirts, often with faces distorted by plastic surgery, walking around with their scantily clad daughters; teenagers covered in tattoos and with noses, ears, eyelids, bellybuttons and tongues littered with metal piercings. Ms. Ingraham rightly states that this is not individual expression.' It is the degradation of the self – the expression of a hedonistic, neo-pagan social order stripped of its Judeo-Christian moorings. The human body is no longer respected but is defamed."[7]

---

[4] The steps from "choose the *church* of your choice" to "choose the *religion* of your choice" to "choose the *lifestyle* of your choice" were short and small.

[5] Fletcher, *Situation Ethics*, 124.

[6] For a report on "Degrading and Non-Degrading Sex in Popular Music: A Content Analysis," by Brian A. Primack (MD, EdM, MS), Melanie A. Gold (DO), Eleanor B. Schwarz (MD, MS), and Madeline A. Dalton (PhD), see *http://www.ncbi.nlm.nih.gov/pmc/articles/PMC2496932/*, accessed 4/3/2014.

[7] Jeffrey T. Kuhner review of Ingraham book, *Of Thee I Zing,* appearing in *The Washington Times,* Nov. 2, 2011. Available online at *http://www.*

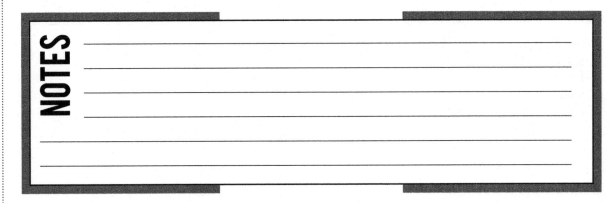

NOTES

Legal decisions have followed the general secular humanist moral movement. Abortion on demand was legalized in the landmark *Roe v. Wade* decision in 1973. Sodomy laws were removed from state laws throughout the last half of the twentieth century; in the 2003 U.S. Supreme Court decision in the *Lawrence v. Texas* case, all remaining state sodomy laws were invalidated. Euthanasia is illegal in all of the United States at the present; however, physician aid in dying (PAD) is now legal in Washington, Oregon, Montana, and Vermont. The key difference between euthanasia and PAD is who administers the lethal dose of medication. Euthanasia entails the physician or another third party administering the medication, whereas PAD requires the patient to self-administer the medication and to determine whether and when to do this. The legal system struggles in defining personhood in areas relating to abortion, stem cell research, reproductive rights, and fetal rights. Belgium's senate approved a measure allowing doctors to euthanize children with disabilities.[8] This is an issue to watch in the future inasmuch as several articles have already appeared defending euthanizing of children.[9]

---

washingtontimes.com/news/2011/nov/2/americas-moral-decline/?page=all, accessed 4/2/2014.

[8] *http://www.lifenews.com/2013/12/12/belgium-senate-approves-measure-allowing-doctors-to-euthanize-children/*, accessed 4/2/2014. In the spring and summer of 1939, Nazis began to organize a secret killing operation that targeted disabled children. At first the program was only for infants and toddlers, but as the scope of program widened it included juveniles up to 17 years old (*http://www.ushmm.org/wlc/en/article.php?ModuleId=10005200*, accessed 4/2/2014).

[9] *http://en.wikipedia.org/wiki/Child_euthanasia*, accessed 4/2/2014.

There is probably little if any disagreement that the morals in America have seen a significant shift in America since the 1960s. Watching the daily news report is enough to alarm many of us.

The Solution to America's Moral Rot Is Not to Be Found in Politics

Robert Bork made this important observation,

But it is well to remember the limits of politics. The political nation is not the same as the cultural nation; the two have different leaders and very different views of the world. Even when conservative political leaders have the votes, liberal cultural leaders operate and exercise influence where votes do not count. However many political victories conservative may produce, they cannot attack modern liberalism in its fortresses. If conservatives come to control the White House and both Houses of Congress, there will be very little change in Hollywood, the network evening news, universities, church bureaucracies, the *New York Times*, or the *Washington Post*. Institutions that are overwhelmingly left-liberal (89 percent of journalists voted for Bill Clinton in 1992) will continue to misinform the public and distort public discourse. The obscenities of popular entertainment will often be protected by the courts. The tyrannies of political correctness and multiculturalism will not be ejected from the universities by any number of conservative victories at the polls. Modern liberals captured the government and its bureaucracies because they captured the culture. Conservative political victories will always be tenuous and fragile unless conservatives recapture the culture.[10]

Frankly, this observation leaves me very discouraged in thinking that America can change the direction of our country. It reminds us of

---

[10] Bork, 339.

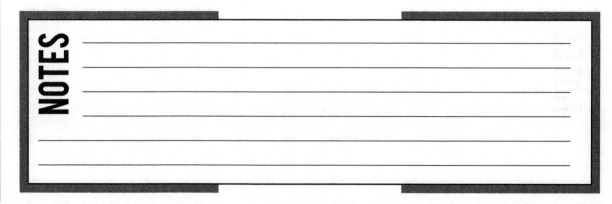

God's warning that He would visit the iniquity of the fathers upon their children unto the third and fourth generation.[11] No political force has the ability and power to redeem a fallen culture.

The Gospel Has Power to Redeem

The only hope for any culture that is in a death spiral because of its moral corruption[12] is in the gospel of Jesus Christ.

God's revelation defines sin. Paul said, "What shall we say then? Is the law sin? Certainly not! On the contrary, I would not have known sin except through the law. For I would not have known covetousness unless the law had said, 'You shall not covet'" (Rom. 7:7). Sin is defined as the transgression of God's law (1 John 3:4). The law, therefore, identifies for us what is right and what is wrong – it defines good and evil. Moses wrote, "I call heaven and earth as witnesses today against you, that I have set before you life and death, blessing and cursing; therefore choose life, that both you and your descendants may live" (Deut. 30:19; cf. 30:15).

The post modern and secular humanist ethics

system eliminates God from its thinking and formulates its ethics independently of revealed religion based on human experience.[13] Their ethics are autonomous (each person decides his own)[14] and situational (right or wrong is determined by the situation, not by divine law).[15]

Some try to define "right" and "wrong" by the community standards in which one lives. If the community approves a given conduct, then it is right to do. Even human experience testifies to what evils this can lead. In Germany in the 1940s, the community decided that ethnic cleansing of the German people was right for the country. The Aryan race was the best and strongest race; the Jews were an inferior race (in fact, so inferior that they were not considered to be "people" by the Nazis). This led to the Holocaust with its gas chambers, which resulted in the murder of 6 million Jews. If you think that ethnic cleansing and genocide were unique to Germany in the 1940s, see how it was used

---

[11] The phrase is repeated in Exodus 20:5; 34:7; Numbers 14:18; Deuteronomy 5:9; and 2 Kings 10:30. The phrase emphasizes that the habits and practices of sin (not its guilt) are transmitted from father to son, being passed down from one generation to the next. We witness this occurring in our own day as well as in Israel's history.

[12] See these passages that describe God's judgment on nations because of their iniquity: Genesis 15:16; Jeremiah 18:6-10; 26:3; Daniel 8:23; Jonah 3:10; Matthew 23:32; 1 Thessalonians 2:16. We also read God's judgment at the Flood (Gen. 6-8) and against Sodom, Gomorrah, and the other cities of the plain (Gen. 19).

[13] Kurtz, *A Secular Humanist Declaration*, 14; *Humanist Manifesto II*, Third article.

[14] Homosexuality is not right for some people; for others it is the lifestyle of choice. In this train of thought, hijacking an airline and flying it into a large building that results in the murder of 3000+ people is not right for some people; for others it is the right thing to do. Autonomous ethics can be described in the words the writer of Judges used to describe those who lived in the period of the judges and acted without regard to a king's law, "In those days there was no king in Israel; everyone did what was right in his own eyes" (Judg. 17:6; 21:25). The law had specifically taught, "You shall not at all do as we are doing here today – every man doing whatever is right in his own eyes" (Deut. 12:8).

[15] Situational ethics states that "murder is usually wrong," but under some situations murder is the loving thing to do; adultery is usually wrong, but under some situations adultery is the loving thing to do.

NOTES

_____
_____
_____
_____
_____
_____

in numerous cases in the twentieth century alone.[16] The world population rather unanimously agrees that the Holocaust, approved by the social environment of the national community in Germany, was wrong. Germany's situational and autonomous ethics are now judged as *wrong*. If there is a *wrong* there must be some measuring stick to determine right from wrong. However, modern ethics would logically have to say, "It is not right for me, but if it is right for them, we cannot judge or condemn them!" (just as we are expected to say about modern homosexuality).

One does not have to wonder what the rejection of God and His word lead to, because God has revealed that for us. Paul wrote in Romans 1:

... although they knew God, they did not glorify Him as God, nor were thankful, but became futile in their thoughts, and their foolish hearts were darkened. Professing to be wise, they became fools, and changed the glory of the incorruptible God into an image made like corruptible man – and birds and four-footed animals and creeping things. Therefore *God also gave them up* to uncleanness, in the lusts of their hearts, to dishonor their bodies among themselves, who exchanged the truth of God for the lie, and worshiped and served the creature rather than the Creator, who is blessed forever. Amen. For this reason *God gave them up* to vile passions. For even their women exchanged the natural use for what is against nature. Likewise also the men, leaving the natural use of the woman, burned in their lust for one another, men with men committing what is shameful, and receiving in themselves the penalty of their error which was due. And even as they did not like to retain God in their knowledge, *God gave them over* to a debased mind, to do those things which are not fitting; being filled with all unrighteousness,

sexual immorality, wickedness, covetousness, maliciousness; full of envy, murder, strife, deceit, evil-mindedness; they are whisperers, backbiters, haters of God, violent, proud, boasters, inventors of evil things, disobedient to parents, undiscerning, untrustworthy, unloving, unforgiving, unmerciful; who, knowing the righteous judgment of God, that those who practice such things are deserving of death, not only do the same but also approve of those who practice them (Rom. 1:21-32).[17]

A better description of what has happened and is continuing to occur in American society could not be written by any sociologist of our own day.

God's revelation provides the motives for righteous living. Not believing in God, why should a person not do what he wants to do? He may reason, "Society will condemn me." But, he replies, "I can commit this act without anyone in society ever knowing." He may think, "The society will throw me in jail." He responds, "I am smart enough to do it without getting caught" or "This provides me so much excitement that I am willing to do the time." He may know his conduct is wrong but argue that the end justifies the means: "The only way I can get out of this ghetto is to sell drugs or rob a bank." He may even defend his conduct saying, "Everyone else is doing it." What motive can one give for not committing the particular act, if ethics is autonomous and situational?

God's revelation responds in at least three ways: (1) There is a final judgment at which time every man will be held accountable for his choices in life; the righteous will be rewarded and the wicked will be punished (Eccl. 12:13-14; Matt.

---

[16] *http://en.wikipedia.org/wiki/Ethnic_cleansing*, accessed 4/3/2014.

[17] Notice Paul's threefold statement that God "gave them up" to immoral conduct as a judgment for their rejecting God from their knowledge (Rom. 1:24, 26, 28).

NOTES
_____
_____
_____
_____
_____
_____

25:1-46; Acts 17:30-31; Rom. 14:12; 2 Cor. 5:10; Rev. 20:11-14). The fear of God persuades man (2 Cor. 5:11). (2) Sin has temporal consequences that make the choice to commit sin irrational.[18] This was the sense in which obedience/disobedience to the will of God was the way of life/death:

> See, I have set before you today life and good, death and evil, in that I command you today to love the LORD your God, to walk in His ways, and to keep His commandments, His statutes, and His judgments, that you may live and multiply; and the LORD your God will bless you in the land which you go to possess. But if your heart turns away so that you do not hear, and are drawn away, and worship other gods and serve them, I announce to you today that you shall surely perish; you shall not prolong your days in the land which you cross over the Jordan to go in and possess (Deut. 30:15-18).

(3) Sin is an offence against God. It grieves the Holy Spirit of God (Eph. 4:30; Isa. 63:10); it wearies Him (Isa. 7:13); causes Him to fret (Ezek. 16:43); grieves Him (Gen. 6:6; Mark 3:5). It drives a wedge of alienation between man and God (Isa. 59:1-2; cf. Gen. 3:8).[19] God's love for His creation motivated Him to act in redeeming mankind from sin: "For God so loved the world that He gave His only begotten Son, that whoever believes in Him should not perish but have everlasting life" (John 3:16). Man reacts in response to God's love: "We love Him because He first loved us" (1 John 4:19). "For

---

[18] Think of the consequences of drunk driving, smoking tobacco, homosexual conduct (AIDS), promiscuous sex (venereal diseases), stealing (incarceration), murder (death penalty), etc.

[19] To understand how sin affects God, think of your reaction to someone sinning against you. It hurts you, alienates you from one another, causes you to fret, and weighs heavily upon your soul.

the love of Christ compels us" (2 Cor. 5:14). Here are motives for humans to make a free-will moral decision to live in compliance with God's universal and absolute moral law.

God redeems mankind. Redemption occurs in two ways: (a) forgiveness and (b) sanctification. Let's look at both: (a) Forgiveness. God has provided a way for sinful man to receive the forgiveness of his sins so that he can be "born again," washed and made clean. Isaiah told his wicked nation,

> Wash yourselves, make yourselves clean; Put away the evil of your doings from before My eyes. Cease to do evil, Learn to do good; Seek justice, Rebuke the oppressor; Defend the fatherless, Plead for the widow. "Come now, and let us reason together," Says the LORD, "Though your sins are like scarlet, They shall be as white as snow; Though they are red like crimson, They shall be as wool. If you are willing and obedient, You shall eat the good of the land; But if you refuse and rebel, You shall be devoured by the sword"; For the mouth of the LORD has spoken (Isa. 1:16-20).

God will do the same for our nation as He was willing to do for Israel. God's nature is what gives one access to His grace. Writing of Israel in the wilderness wanderings, Nehemiah said, "They refused to obey, And they were not mindful of Your wonders That You did among them. But they hardened their necks, And in their rebellion They appointed a leader To return to their bondage. But You are God, Ready to pardon, Gracious and merciful, Slow to anger, Abundant in kindness, And did not forsake them" (Neh. 9:17; cf. Exod. 34:6; Num. 14:18; 2 Chron. 30:9; Pss. 86:15; 103:8; etc.). God's grace toward mankind is still willing to forgive sins.

NOTES
_____
_____
_____
_____
_____
_____
_____

(b) Sanctification. The soul whom God has purified is taught to cleanse himself from sin. For example, Paul wrote,

> But you have not so learned Christ, if indeed you have heard Him and have been taught by Him, as the truth is in Jesus: that you put off, concerning your former conduct, the old man which grows corrupt according to the deceitful lusts, and be renewed in the spirit of your mind, and that you put on the new man which was created according to God, in true righteousness and holiness. Therefore, putting away lying, "Let each one of you speak truth with his neighbor," for we are members of one another. "Be angry, and do not sin": do not let the sun go down on your wrath, nor give place to the devil. Let him who stole steal no longer, but rather let him labor, working with his hands what is good, that he may have something to give him who has need. Let no corrupt word proceed out of your mouth, but what is good for necessary edification, that it may impart grace to the hearers. And do not grieve the Holy Spirit of God, by whom you were sealed for the day of redemption. Let all bitterness, wrath, anger, clamor, and evil speaking be put away from you, with all malice. And be kind to one another, tenderhearted, forgiving one another, just as God in Christ forgave you (Eph. 4:20-32).[20]

The gospel can take a drunkard, drug abuser, thief, fornicator, homosexual, etc. and make him a new creature in Christ, sanctified and suitable for the Master's use (2 Tim. 2:21).

Conclusion

The means of redeeming the nation is the gospel. It cannot be done nationally (as if one could baptize the American nation); it must be done one soul at a time. Just as the corruption of our nation has occurred one soul at a time until it spread through the culture, so also the redemption of America can only occur through the process of preaching the gospel to honest hearted souls and allowing its leaven to work in the society in which we live. Before you say that this is such a monumental task that it can never be accomplished, remember that twelve disciples started out on a mission on the day of Pentecost. The world in which they lived differed little from that in which we live today. The gospel changed the world without the use of the printed media, radio, TV, or internet that allows it to be more quickly disseminated. How dare we despair or be discouraged in the face of our responsibility to take the gospel to men in our age! Remember Moses's words to Joshua: "Be strong and of a good courage: for thou must go with this people unto the land which the LORD hath sworn unto their fathers to give them; and thou shalt cause them to inherit it. And the LORD, He it is that doth go before thee; He will be with thee, He will not fail thee, neither forsake thee: fear not, neither be dismayed" (Deut. 31:7-8).

---

[20] For other texts showing this sanctification, consider: John 17:17; Romans 12:1-21; 1 Corinthians 6:9-11; Galatians 5:16-26; Colossians 3:1-17; etc.

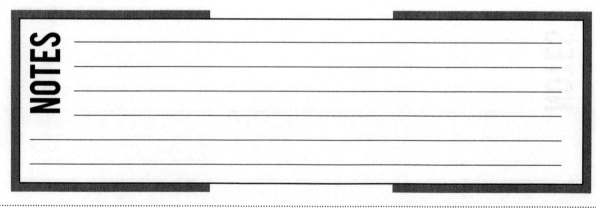

Questions

1. Talk with one older member of your congregation to ask him how moral values have shifted within his lifetime. Are his views similar to those described in this lesson? _____ _____

2. What is "situational ethics"? _____ _____

3. What does the atheist mean when he says ethics are "autonomous"? _____ _____

4. After fifty years, how would you judge the fruit of humanist ethics? _____ _____

5. Why can't political elections solve American moral problems?_____ _____

6. What does Exodus 20:5 mean when it says that God visits "the iniquity of the fathers upon the children unto the third and fourth generation of them that hate me"?_____ _____

7. What do these verses teach about how God acts toward the wickedness of a nation: Genesis 15:16; Jeremiah 18:6-10; Jonah 3:10?_____ _____

8. How does a Christian determine what is sinful?_____ _____

9. How is the escalation of wickedness tied to rejection of God and His word, according to Romans 1:18-32? _____ _____

10. What motives does humanist ethics give for more virtuous living? _____ _____

11. What motives does the gospel give for godly living (provide Scriptures with your answers)?

    a._____

    b._____

    c._____

NOTES
_____
_____
_____
_____
_____
_____

12. How does the gospel redeem man?

a._____

b._____

13. How does forgiveness change man? _____

_____

14. How does sanctification change man? _____

_____

15. How is forgiveness grounded in the nature of God (Neh. 9:17)? _____

_____

NOTES
_____
_____
_____
_____
_____
_____

The Church

Previously we considered the role of "church and state" but this chapter will take us in a different direction. In this chapter, we want to look at how pluralism, with its newly defined definition of tolerance, has invaded and affected the church. I will be looking at the "church" in two senses: (a) religious groups that claim some type of faith in Jesus; (b) the local churches following the New Testament pattern. We will consider how pluralism affects the religious leadership and morality of denominations, their religious schools, preaching, evangelism, and the gospel's exclusive message.

Secular Humanism and the Religious leadership

Secular humanists have long recognized that many of the denominational religious leadership have accepted the same viewpoints that they themselves hold. *Humanist Manifesto I* (1933) called for religious institutions to change: "Certainly religious institutions, their ritualistic forms, ecclesiastical methods, and communal activities must be reconstituted as rapidly as experience allows, in order to function effectively in the modern world." By the time of the writing of *Humanist Manifesto II* (1973), humanists were able to say, "Many within religious groups, believing in the future of humanism, now claim humanist credentials. Humanism is an ethical process through which we all can move, above and beyond the divisive particulars, heroic personalities, dogmatic creeds, and ritual customs of past religions or their mere negation."

Robert H. Bork wrote, "What Frederic Lewis Allen noted of the 1920s was true for a long time previously and remains true today: religion is declining because those identified with it do not actually believe in it."[1] Bork charged that the churches have turned left.[2] The National Council of Churches of Christ in the United States (NCC), which represents mainline Protestant denominations, consistently has taken left positions. The World Council of Churches (WCC) is even worse, usually supporting pro-Communist views and anti-United States stances.[3]

What Has Been the Influence of Pluralism on Evangelical Churches?

Josh McDowell and Bob Hostetler also showed how pluralism has invaded the Evangelical churches. Consider the following statistics:

---

[1] Robert H. Bork, *Slouching Toward Gomorrah,* 280. The quotation is taken from Frederic Lewis Allen, *Only Yesterday: An Informal History of the 1920's* (New York: Harper & Row, 1959), 164.

[2] *Ibid.,* 282.

[3] *Op.cit.,* 283.

Before and After	
What is your reaction to a sermon that contrasts error and truth? Are you uncomfortable because it might cause some visitor not to return?	
Before	**After**

- Fifty-seven percent of *churched youth* do not believe an objective standard of truth exists;
- Almost as many Bible-believing, conservative *Christian adults* – 53 percent – do not believe in absolute truth
- Eighty-four percent of first-year *Christian college students* cannot intelligently defend or explain their beliefs
- Two-thirds of the 70 percent of Americans who say it is important to follow the teachings of the Bible *reject moral absolutes.[4]*

One has only to visit various denominational web sites to see what they believe or do not believe.

The Modern Church and Morality

Until the 1950s, most Protestant and Catholic denominations were positively influencing American society in respect to moral ethics. Generally, they taught biblical morality. This is no longer so.[5]

Twenty-first century mainline denominations parrot the moral standards of the political left.

[4] Josh McDowell and Bob Hostetler, *The New Tolerance*, 173-174.

[5] I need to acknowledge that these are general statements; there are some conservative Evangelical churches that teach basic Bible morality, but they are in the minority. Generally, however, American churches have left what the Bible teaches in order to become "relevant." What I am saying about this shift in teaching Biblical morality among modern denominations is not true of every individual in it. Some members of these denominations are in the same situation as righteous Lot whose soul was vexed daily by the ungodliness he saw in Sodom and Gomorrah (2 Pet. 2:7). Please understand that I am not indicting every individual in these denominations when I chronicle the moral decline in the denominations.

They condemn bigotry toward homosexuals (homophobia) and warn of the dangers of radical religious fundamentalists who protest abortion and bomb abortion clinics, oppose no-fault divorce, deny medical benefits for live-in lovers; etc. These denominations have accepted the world's standards as their own in many of their beliefs. Even Evangelical Christians dress as immodestly as the world, see nothing wrong with drinking intoxicating beverages (so long as one does not drive while drinking) and smoking marijuana, think gambling is innocent recreation (some churches even use gambling as fund raisers), and accept practicing fornicators (it is thought to be normal for teens to be sexually active) and those who have divorced for causes other than fornication and remarried into their fellowship.

The abortion conflict shows the influence of secular humanism on American churches. The 1973 Supreme Court decision in the *Roe v. Wade* case legalized abortion in America; however this decision does not mean that God approves of abortion. One would think that the church would be a bastion of righteousness defending the lives of the unborn babies in the womb. Unfortunately this has not been the case. The Roman Catholic Church and most Evangelical churches have consistently condemned abortion. However, mainline Protestant churches have taken the opposite stance, defending a woman's right to kill her unborn child.[6]

Also enlightening is the on-going evolution of the church's stance on homosexuality. The

[6] "Conservative Protestants tend to be anti-abortion whereas 'mainline' Protestants lean towards an abortion-rights stance. African-American Protestants are much more strongly anti-abortion than white Protestants" (*http://en.wikipedia.org/wiki/Christianity_and_abortion#Range_of_positions_taken_by_Christian_denominations*, accessed 4/7/2014).

NOTES

_____

_____

_____

_____

_____

_____

Old Testament clearly condemns homosexuality (Gen. 19:4-10;[7] Lev. 18:22-23; 20:13; Deut. 23:17; 1 Kings 14:24; 15:12; 22:46; 23:7); it is joined with bestiality as an abomination of the pagans (Exod. 22:19; Lev. 20:15-16; Deut. 27:21). The New Testament teaching is equally as clear (see Rom. 1:24-27; 1 Cor. 6:9-11; 1 Tim. 1:10). Despite the clarity and uniformity of teaching on homosexuality, mainline Protestant denominations are dividing over whether or not to appoint homosexuals as preachers/ministers.[8]

---

[7] The attempted homosexual rape episode in Genesis 19 is described in the New Testament as the unrighteous deeds of the ungodly (2 Pet. 2:6), the filthy conversation of the wicked (2 Pet. 2:7), unlawful deeds (2 Pet. 2:8), and fornication and "strange flesh" (Jude 7).

[8] See *http://en.wikipedia.org/wiki/List_of_Christian_denominational_positions_on_homosexuality* (accessed 4/7/2014) for a summary of denominational positions on homosexuality.

Churches opposed: Seventh Day Adventists, Baptist (some American Baptist Churches are tolerant of homosexuality); Churches of Christ (with this significant additional comment: "Some Churches of Christ are beginning to address this issue with an open and compassionate approach. Several universities associated with the fellowship have held forums and conferences to address the issue and to open up discussion on the approach Christians should take toward homosexuality."); Jehovah's Witnesses; Pentecostal; Roman Catholic; Nazarene; Latter Day Saints; Lutheran Church (Missouri Synod).

Churches supportive: Anglican and Episcopal (the result of supporting homosexuality led to the forming in 2008 of the Fellowship of Confessing Anglicans, representing two-thirds of all Anglicans); Lutheran; Presbyterian (though some smaller groups condemn homosexual behavior); Quakers; Eastern Orthodox; United Methodist; United Church of Christ; United Reformed Church; Disciples of Christ.

Several churches are **conflicted**, with groups

Infidelity at the Religious Colleges

One would expect that the public schools, controlled by secular humanists, would be teaching secular humanist values. However, most Christians would probably be surprised to learn what is being taught in "Christian" seminaries across America (as well as in Europe). Ken Ham and Greg Hall published *Already Compromised*, a book designed to show that many Evangelical colleges are already compromised on the core issues of Christianity. The book opens with a brief recounting of how the religious Ivy League schools (Harvard, Yale, Princeton, Dartmouth) had been established to teach Christian values but were taken over by liberals who denied miracles, the inspiration of Scripture, and the deity of Christ. Then Ham raised the question, "Is history repeating itself?" Ham and Hall assert that an "uncertain sound" is emanating from many of our religious colleges and added, "The authority of Scripture is being undermined at many levels, and the voices of naturalism, agnosticism, and even atheism are permeating the eardrums of generations of young people who become the leaders of tomorrow."[9] Ham and Hall cite statistics of questions asked of over 200 religious colleges and universities from across America to show how infidelity has already infiltrated the campuses of religious colleges.

The Influence of Pluralism on Preaching

Let's review what pluralism is. Pluralism denies that there are any absolutes in either morals or truth claims. Relativism believes that all religions

---

splintering off because of the majority decisions to support homosexuality.

[9] Ken Ham and Greg Hall, *Already Compromised*, 13.

NOTES

_____
_____
_____
_____
_____
_____

are of equal value, in spite of their contradictory truth claims, and that none of the religions give access to absolute truth. Early twentieth century churches took an ecumenical stance[10] toward each other; the various denominations began recognizing as Christians those within other fellowships, without regard to the differences in their beliefs. As religious liberalism (denial of the inspiration of Scripture, denial of miracles, deity of Christ, etc.) took control of the denominations, Evangelicals could not tolerate those who denied inspiration, miracles, and the deity of Christ. New fellowships were formed along the watershed issues of inspiration of the Scriptures, miracles, and the deity of Christ. These were doctrines *fundamental* to Christianity (hence, the word "Fundamentalists" was used to describe these groups).

However, these groups did not remove the residing virus that was destroying their denominations. They adhered to the poisonous ecumenical doctrine of unity in doctrinal diversity, justifying that stance by asserting that we must be united in the gospel but allow room for doctrinal differences. The Fundamentalists were able to tolerate *doctrinal* differences so long as one was preaching the *gospel*. As time passed, what was included in "gospel" was progressively reduced and what was included in "doctrine" was increased. This allowed interdenominational fellowship but undermined commitment to revealed truth. If one could fellowship someone who taught non-Biblical doctrine on the organization of the church, why not fellowship others who were mistaken about the virgin birth? The ecumenical spirit was alive and well

––––––––––

[10] Ecumenism is an approach to unity among Christian churches that recognizes that all denominations are acceptable to God, despite their denominational differences.

within the Fundamentalist movement, just one generation behind their more liberal mainline Protestant cousins.

Ecumenism, and subsequently pluralism, in society exalted toleration as the only absolute virtue.[11] Pluralism's denial of any absolute truths means that one has to accept as equally valid all truth claims. The "truth claim" that the "world is flat" is just as valid as the truth claim that the earth is an oblate spheroid (or ellipsoid).[12] According to pluralism, the truth claim of a group that teaches that Jesus was an illegitimate son of two first century peasants is equally valid as a group that teaches that Jesus was born of a virgin. When pluralists speak of "tolerance" they mean the recognition that both truth claims are equally valid, not that one tolerates another preaching his mistaken views. The pluralist view of tolerance leads to the conclusion that nothing is true and nothing is false. If there is no true and false, there is no orthodoxy and no heresy.[13]

The acceptance of pluralism has reshaped gospel preaching. Even those who are not religious leaders have noticed the change in the content of preaching. In *Slouching Toward Gomorrah*, Robert H. Bork commented about the shift in content in gospel preaching:

> It is not helpful that the ideas of salvation and damnation, of sin and virtue, which once

––––––––––

[11] "...the primary 'moral' line drawn through Western culture declares that those who 'tolerate' just about anything are good, and those who do not are bad and therefore should not be tolerated'" (D. A. Carson, *The Intolerance of Tolerance,* 134).

[12] This means that instead of being of equal circumference in all areas, the poles are squished, resulting in a bulge at the equator, and thus a larger circumference and diameter there.

[13] See D. A. Carson, *The Gagging of God*, 175.

NOTES

_____

_____

_____

_____

_____

_____

_____

played major roles in Christian belief, are now almost never heard of in the mainline churches. The sermons and homilies are now almost exclusively about love, kindness, and eternal life. That may be regarded, particularly by the sentimental, as an improvement in humaneness, indeed in civility, but it also means an alteration in the teaching of Christianity that makes the religion less powerful as a moral force.[14]

D. A. Carson noted the same shift in preaching as he spoke of the preaching of American televangelist Robert Schuller (1926 – 2015) who spoke on the *Hour of Prayer* and was the founder of the Crystal Cathedral in Garden Grove, CA where it was broadcast. Carson wrote,

> Consider how many "conservatives" enjoy Robert Schuller. That brand of "gospel" cannot last. Weigh how many presentations of the gospel have been "eased" by portraying Jesus as the One who fixes marriages, ensures the American dream, cancels loneliness, gives us power, and generally makes us happy.[15]

Carson bluntly stated, "If you begin with perceived needs, you will always distort the gospel. If you begin with the Bible's definition of our need, relating perceived needs to that central grim reality, you are more likely to retain intact the gospel of God."[16]

Changes in Preaching among the Churches of Christ

The impact of the positive preaching movement in America on preaching among the churches of Christ has been observed by historians among us. Richard T. Hughes described the reaction to Foy E. Wallace's

exposure of premillennialism in the churches of Christ in the 1930s. Those who reacted negatively to Wallace's writings and preaching "increasingly called for positive thinking, positive preaching, and positive writing. ... this emphasis on positive thinking increasingly became a hallmark of the progressive leadership of Churches of Christ."[17] Hughes also described the change that occurred in the content of the *Herald of Truth* radio and television programs in the 1950s-1970s. Competing against Joshua Liebman's *Peace of Mind* (1946), Fulton Sheen's *Peace of Soul* (1949), and Norman Vincent Peale's *Power of Positive Thinking* (1952), the leaders of *Herald of Truth* realized that their message had to change.

> In such a climate, messages that extolled the "true church" and that condemned "the denominations" for their "false doctrine" were not likely to develop a significant following beyond the ranks of the faithful. This ministry was at a crossroads: it could continue to preach to the converted or it could seek to extend its reach. But if Churches of Christ wanted to reach out, conventional wisdom suggested that they could not expect to compete effectively in the denominational free market of souls unless they embraced the sort of "peace-of-mind" piety that dominated the national religious landscape for more than a decade.[18]

Batsel Barrett Baxter, the speaker for *Herald of Truth*,

> ... continued to preach on the traditional themes pertaining to the Church of Christ identity, to be sure, but he also introduced subtle shifts in emphasis that would be far-reaching in their impact on Churches of Christ. With increasing frequency, he explained to the national radio or television audiences, how to achieve spiritual

---

[14] Bork, 293.

[15] Carson, *The Gagging of God,* 221.

[16] *Ibid.*

---

[17] Richard T. Hughes, *Reviving the Ancient Faith*, 191.

[18] *Ibid.*, 241.

NOTES

_____
_____
_____
_____
_____
_____

growth and peace of mind, how to develop healthy family relationships, and how to cope with anxiety and fear or with the various stages along life's way."[19]

Positive thinking preaching has been dominant in institutional churches for about fifty years, resulting in the situation that modern institutional churches of Christ are presently in conflict over whether to move into the mainstream of Protestant denominationalism or adhere to their loyalty to Jesus Christ.[20] In spite of the damage that has been historically documented among our institutional brethren, there is among non-institutional churches a distinctive movement toward positive preaching that shuns preaching on the identity of the local church and exposing the false doctrines of denominationalism, that avoids preaching on issues of modesty, social drinking, gambling, and other issues pertaining to sanctification, and highlights the emphasis on Christianity as a way to find inner peace of mind. The effect of fifty years of such preaching among us will be the same as it has had among institutional churches – a generation will rise up who cannot distinguish the Lord's church from Protestant denominationalism.

Pluralism Destroys Evangelism

Pluralists believe that the truth claims of all religions are equal in value and that none of

the religions gives access to absolute and total religious truth. To put this in the perspective of Biblical times, to the pluralist the worship of Baal, Diana of the Ephesians, and Jehovah are all equally valid. In modern parlance, one denomination is no better than another. Mormonism's Adam-God doctrine ("as man is, God once was; as God is, man may be")[21] and Jehovah's Witnesses' belief that Jesus is "a god" are to be treated as equally true as the teaching of Scripture on these subjects. And, more recently, the trend has been that all of the world religions are equally valid. Buddhism, Hinduism, Islam, secular religions, animism, and Christianity are equally legitimate and one religion must not condemn another religion.

Beliefs have consequences and one of the consequences of this form of relativism is that it is increasingly considered inappropriate to try to change someone else's mind on his religious beliefs. S. D. Gaede made this observation.

These days it is a scary thing to stand face to face with another person and suggest that their ideas may be wrong. So we try to be as indirect as possible, laying out the gospel message in a way that will sound attractive to the modern ear. Even then, however, it is scary business. Sit down with a group of evangelicals these days and you will discover that they are petrified to express their faith. How odd, we may think, since they live in a society where such freedom is protected by law. But their reticence is not odd at all when we consider that one of our culture's deepest values is tolerance, and that value is embedded in a relativistic worldview. To assert

---

[19] Hughes, *op. cit.*, 241.

[20] The issues presently under discussion include: (1) Is baptism for the remission of sins? (2) Should instruments of music be used in the worship of the church? (3) What is the role of women in public services? (4) What is Jesus's teaching on divorce and remarriage? (4) Does the Holy Spirit operate apart from God's word? (5) Is theistic evolution compatible with the Bible? (6) Does the Bible allow the following in worship: use of drama teams, hand clapping, special Easter/Christmas services; etc.?

---

[21] James E. Talmage, *Articles of Faith,* Ch. 24, pp. 430-431; Lorenzo Snow (1898-1901), *The Teaching of Lorenzo Snow,* ed. Clyde J. Williams (1984), 1; Bruce McConkie, *Mormon Doctrine*, 237.

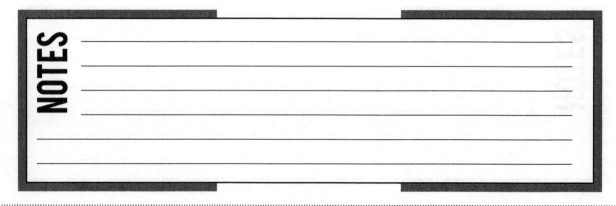

NOTES

truth in such an environment is blasphemy. Evangelists are the heretics of our age.[22]

In American society, where religion is privatized, someone who publicly preaches his views about religion is violating cultural norms. Everyone's religion is his own personal choice; one should no more try to change a person's choice in religion than he should speak to a stranger going through a buffet line to persuade him to chose fried chicken instead of roast beef. Were he to do the latter, he would promptly be told to mind his own business and to back off.

How does one distinguish "evangelism" from "proyselyting"? Some Christians define "proselytism" as the attempt to convert people from one Christian denomination to another; those who use the term in this way generally view the practice as illegitimate and in contrast to evangelism, which is converting non-Christians to Christianity. To Christians, those who are in unauthorized "Christian" denominations are just as lost as those in unrevealed world religions, so evangelism includes taking the gospel to those lost ones in American denominations as well as to secularists and those involved in world religions. Jesus's charge to evangelize the lost included the lost sheep of the house of Israel (Matt. 10:6) as well as the Gentiles;[23] in the same way, His charge to evangelize today includes those lost ones attending denominations founded and governed by men. The term "proselyting" is being used in a pejorative way to condemn what the Bible calls "evangelism." In several countries

(mostly under Muslim domination), trying to get someone to convert from his native faith is a punishable offence.

Given the antagonism of the courts, Hollywood, and news media toward Christianity, America might soon have a value system that is similar to the first century Roman empire in which "intolerance toward Christians was widely perceived as a virtue."[24]

Pluralism Destroys the Gospel's Exclusive Message

What made Christianity grow into a world religion was its unique message. Early Christians unabashedly proclaimed that salvation is only available through the crucified and risen Savior, Jesus Christ. Here are some of its exclusivistic texts:

> Therefore I said to you that you will die in your sins; for if you do not believe that I am He, you will die in your sins (John 8:24).

> Jesus said to him, "I am the way, the truth, and the life. No one comes to the Father except through Me" (John 14:6).

> And He said to them, "Go into all the world and preach the gospel to every creature. He who believes and is baptized will be saved; but he who does not believe will be condemned" (Mark 16:15-16).

> Nor is there salvation in any other, for there is no other name under heaven given among men by which we must be saved (Acts 4:12).

---

[22] S. D. Gaede, *When Tolerance Is No Virtue*, 45.

[23] Paul's usual pattern was to go first into the synagogue to teach and then turn to the Gentiles (Acts 13:14-14, 42-46; 14:1; 17:1, 10, 17; 18:4, 19; cf. Rom. 1:16). Was Paul proselytizing Jews and Gentile "God-fearers"?

[24] The situation of the early Roman empire was so described by D. A. Carson, *The Intolerance of Tolerance*, 53. Also, see chapter on "The Privatization of Faith" for the process by which evangelism has become a dirty word.

NOTES

Demetrius, the Ephesian silversmith, understood the preaching of Paul when he said, "this Paul has persuaded and turned away many people, saying that they are not gods which are made with hands" (Acts 19:26). Paul had written the Corinthians saying, "we know that an idol is nothing in the world, and that there is no other God but one. For even if there are so-called gods, whether in heaven or on earth (as there are many gods and many lords), yet for us there is one God, the Father, of whom are all things, and we for Him; and one Lord Jesus Christ, through whom are all things, and through whom we live" (1 Cor. 8:4-6). Throughout both Testaments, the worship of other gods is condemned[25] and idolatry is forbidden.[26] The New Testament affirms that there is one God (Eph. 4:6).

The New Testament's exclusive message is diametrically opposed to the mantra of pluralism. First of all, the New Testament affirms (a) that there is a body of revealed truth, (b) that it can be understood, and (c) that salvation is conditional upon correctly understanding that truth. Jesus Himself said, "And you shall know the truth, and the truth shall make you free" (John 8:32). Secondly, Jesus did not believe that every value system and truth claim was equally valid or that it is valid for one social community but not another. The same gospel was to be preached to every creature under heaven (Mark 16:15-16; Acts 17:30-31). Those systems that oppose the gospel are invalid, untrue, wrong, and sinful, even though there are some elements of truth in each of them. Men are called out of these belief systems of darkness and into God's marvelous light as shown in the gospel (Col. 1:13).[27]

Michael Babcock explained why the early church grew so rapidly, drawing from E. R. Dodds' *Pagan and Christian in an Age of Anxiety* (Cambridge: Cambridge University Press, 1991). He listed these four reasons:[28]

1. The exclusiveness of the Christian message.

2. The *inclusiveness* of the Christian message. By this Babcock means that the gospel is available to all of mankind; there are no caste systems in the church.

3. The *other worldliness* of the message. "In a time when earthly life was increasingly devalued and guilt-feelings were widely prevalent, Christianity held out to the disinherited the conditional promise of a better inheritance in another world."[29]

4. The *benefits* of becoming a Christian were not confined to the next world. Christians fostered a sense of community, a *belongingness* that displays itself in social responsibility.

To the degree that these messages are compromised, the effectiveness of the Lord's people in evangelism is hampered, according to Babcock.

---

[25] See Exodus 20:3; Deuteronomy 5:7; 6:14; 2 Kings 17:35; Jeremiah 25:6; 35:15.

[26] See Exodus 20:4; Leviticus 26:1; Deuteronomy 4:15-19; 5:8; 27:15; Psalm 97:7. For New Testament condemnations of idolatry, see Acts 17:16; 1 Corinthians 6:9-11; 10:7, 14; Galatians 5:20; Colossians 3:5; Revelation 21:8; 22:15.

[27] For example, Paul spoke of the conversion of the Thessalonians saying, "For they themselves declare concerning us what manner of entry we had to you, and how you turned to God from idols to serve the living and true God, and to wait for His Son from heaven, whom He raised from the dead, even Jesus who delivers us from the wrath to come" (1 Thess. 1:9-10).

[28] Babcock, *Unchristian America*, 150-156.

[29] *Ibid.*, 153. Babcock is quoting from Dodds.

Conclusion

This chapter has discussed how pluralism has infiltrated the modern denominations, causing many to reject Biblical absolutist statements. Churches have been compromised both in morals and doctrinal beliefs. Gospel preaching has become impotent "be good, do good" homilies that are non-judgmental of anyone's beliefs or behavior. We also pointed out how the positive preaching movement affected institutional churches of Christ and is penetrating non-institutional churches. As pluralism gains acceptance evangelism wanes – indeed, it becomes a "dirty" word. The cessation of distinctive gospel preaching is a symptom of a weak and dying church. In reaction to this, Christians should get back to first-century preaching to overcome the influences of twenty-first century pluralism in our society and in our churches.

Questions

1. Why do atheists say many of the religious leadership agree with them? _____
   _____

2. Cite evidences that show American churches have quit teaching against immorality. _____
   _____

3. What is happening to religious colleges in the wake of the infidelity that is sweeping through America?_____
   _____

4. Why are questions such as "What is the age of the earth?", "Was the Genesis Flood a universal flood?", and "How long were the days of creation?" important to ask when choosing a religious college? _____
   _____

5. What do Fundamentalist/Evangelical churches believe in contrast to mainstream denominations?
   _____
   _____

6. Why is the "gospel" and "doctrine" distinction important for Evangelicals?_____
   _____
   _____

7. Why is "tolerance" such an important issue for post-modernists? _____
   _____

NOTES
_____
_____
_____
_____
_____

8. How has post-modernism affected gospel preaching ...

   a. Among denominations? _____

   b. Among institutional churches? _____

   c. Among non-institutional churches? _____

9. What has been the consequence of these changes in ...

   a. Mainline denominations? _____

   _____

   b. Institutional churches? _____

   _____

   c. Non-institutional churches? _____

   _____

10. What is proselyting? Why do most churches believe it is evil? _____

   _____

11. Why is evangelism considered an evil by post-modernism? _____

   _____

12. What does one mean when he says Christianity is *exclusive*? _____

   _____

13. What does one mean when he says Christianity is *inclusive*? _____

   _____

14. Cite two texts that demonstrate the exclusive claims of Christianity. _____

   _____

15. What four reasons did E. R. Dodds list for the rapid growth of the early church?

   a. _____

   b. _____

   c. _____

   d. _____

NOTES

_____

_____

_____

_____

_____

Sexuality

Ancient cultures had their fertility gods and goddesses, such as Hittite (Shaushka), Canaanite (Baal), Egyptian (16 deities), Philistine (Dagon), Babylonian (Ishtar, Nanshe, and lesser deities), Greek (Aphrodite, Adonis, Demeter, Dionysius, Eros, Persephone and 13 other deities), Roman (Diana, Venus, and 27 others), and many others.[1] Religious rituals reenacted, either actually or symbolically, sexual acts and/or reproductive processes. Max Weber wrote, "Sexual intoxication is a typical component of the orgy ... rites of the various functional gods who control reproduction, whether of man, beast, cattle, or grains of seed."[2] The ancient Israelites confronted the sexual deities of their day, just as we must today.[3]

This lesson will show how America has made sex a god in in modern society. We will show how media has contributed to the prevailing hedonism in modern culture and then contrast sexuality in modern culture with sexuality according to the Bible.

In many respects, America treats sex as one of its idols. In 1965, Harvey Cox observed how *Miss America* and *Playboy* become the "pagan deities" – the god and his consort – of American culture. *Miss America* plays the role of defining a young woman's identity, and becomes the tool to market almost every thing our consumer society markets, according to Cox. The god *Playboy* is the counterpart to *Miss America*. For *Playboy*, "Sex becomes one of the items of leisure activity that the knowledgeable consumer of leisure handles with his characteristic skill and detachment." The girl becomes a desirable – indeed an indispensable – "Playboy accessory." The girl becomes a "thing." For *Playboy* sex is "always a casual but satisfying sexual experience with no entangling alliances whatever."[4] What Cox described in *The Secular City* is reality.

---

[1] *http://en.wikipedia.org/wiki/List_of_fertility_deities.*

[2] Weber, *The Sociology of Religion*, 236.

[3] The Israelites were tempted to assimilate the worship of the cultures around them. The various male gods surrounding Israel were as follows: Phoenician: Baal; Ammon: Milkom; Moab: Chemesh; Philistine: Dagon and later Baal. But for all of these, the female consort was Asherah. Significantly, the "Israelite sanctuary at Kuntillet 'Ajrud in the Sinai, dating to the late ninth or early eighth century B.C.E., ... refer(s) to Yahweh 'and his Asherah.' This site of course is outside the borders of Judah. But a reference to the divine couple has also been found at the site of Khirbet el-Kom, in the heart of Judah (near Hebron). A tomb inscription there reads: "Blessed will be Ariyahu to Yahweh and

his Asherah." These Israelite apostasies at Kuntillet 'Ajrud and Khirbet el-Kom are illustrations of how Israel assimilated pagan practices in her own people and worship.

[4] Harvey Cox, *The Secular City*, 167-189.

Before and After	
How would you react?	
Your college student son has started living together with his girlfriend. When they come home for Christmas, they expect to sleep together in your house.	
Before	**After**

"Hookup sex" has become commonplace in American culture.[5] Sex without commitment is emotionally more exacting on women than men. Kelly O'Connell explained,

> The emotional harm suffered is more long-lasting and deeper in women than men because of profound differences between the two sexes in how sexual relations are experienced. Stepp describes how typical it is for young women to get involved with a man sexually and then become devastated when he is uninterested in a post-hookup relationship. This persists despite the understood ground rules, yet these women are often torn apart by the experience.[6]

The influence of secularism is particularly witnessed in the sexual revolution that began in the 1960s and dominates America's culture in the twenty-first century. The secular approach to sex behavior is evident from the *Humanist Manifesto II* and *A Secular Humanist Declaration*.

> *Humanist Manifesto II:* In the area of sexuality, we believe that intolerant attitudes, often cultivated by orthodox religions and puritanical cultures, unduly repress sexual conduct. ... While we do not approve of exploitive, denigrating forms of sexual expression, neither do we wish to prohibit, by law or social sanction, sexual behavior between consenting adults. The many varieties of sexual exploration should not in themselves be considered "evil." Without countenancing mindless permissiveness or unbridled promiscuity, a civilized society should be a tolerant one. Short of harming others or compelling them to do likewise, individuals should be permitted to express their sexual proclivities and pursue their lifestyles as they desire. We wish to cultivate the development of a responsible attitude toward sexuality, in which humans are not exploited as sexual objects, and in which intimacy, sensitivity, respect, and honesty in interpersonal relations are encouraged. Moral education for children and adults is an important way of developing awareness and sexual maturity.[7]

> *A Secular Humanist Declaration:* "Nor do we believe that any one church should impose its view of moral virtue and sin, sexual conduct, marriage, divorce, birth control, or abortion, or legislate them for the rest of society" (15).

The prevailing cultural view of sex is that anything two consenting adults agree upon is acceptable sexuality.

Robert H. Bork commented on recreational sex as portrayed in American society as follows:

> Recreational sex, for example, is pervasive and is presented as acceptable about six times as often as it is rejected. Homosexuals and prostitutes are shown as social victims. Television takes a neutral attitude towards adultery, prostitution, and pornography. It "warns against the dangers of imposing the majority's restrictive sexual morality on these practices. The villains in TV's moralist plays are not deviants and libertines but puritans and prudes." The moral relativism of the Sixties is now television's public morality.[8]

---

[5] "Hook ups" are unplanned sexual encounters, usually fueled by alcohol.

[6] Kelly O'Connell, "Careless Love: Hookup Sex Culture a Symbol of America's Declining Character," *Canada Free Press* (July 17, 2012). Available online at *http://www.canadafreepress.com/index.php/article/48062*, accessed 4/14/2014.

[7] Humanists speak of forms of sexual misconduct that are "evil." The moral imperative (ought, should) appears in their statements. What moral standard is there in the humanist system that determines what is good and evil, what one should and should not do? What one views as "exploitive" is another's alternate lifestyle.

[8] Bork, *Slouching Toward Gomorrah,* 127. The sentences cited in quotation marks are from *Prime*

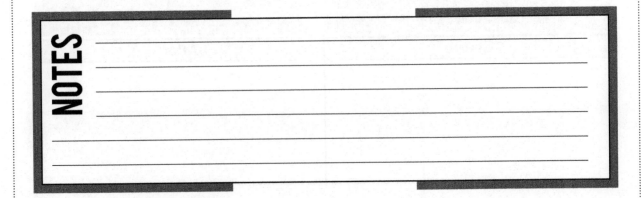

NOTES

That Bork's statement is not off base is seen from the opening comments of the research team from Elon University in Elon, NC: "Popular culture has belittled the moral significance of sexual relations among young Americans, and the idea that sex is merely a recreational activity has prevailed. Whether or not this is a respectable mindset is a debatable, but also separate, issue; the existence of this mindset among adolescent Americans is unquestionable."[9]

At the conclusion of his chapter on sex, Bork stated,

> Reflecting on where we have come, Maggie Gallagher wrote: "Sex was remade in the image of Hugh Hefner; Eros demoted from a god to a buffoon. Over the last thirty years, America transformed itself into a pornographic culture." Gallagher accepted Angela Carter's definition, stated in somewhat more basic Anglo-Saxon, that pornography is basically propaganda for fornication, and offered a definition of her own: "[A] pornographic culture is not one in which pornographic materials are published and distributed. A pornographic culture is one which accepts the ideas about sex on which pornography is based."[10]

Time: How TV Portrays American Culture, by S. Robert Lichter, Linda S. Lichter, and Stanley Rotham (Washington, DC: Regnery Publishing, 1994), 416.

[9] "Perceptions of Sexuality in American Culture," Research Team: Kathryn Dykeman, Damon Duncan, Kristen Irvin, and Amber King. Available online at *http://org.elon.edu/summit/essays/essay9.pdf*, accessed 4/14/2014. The recommendations provided in this report are the typical approach presented by liberals – sex education (but not abstinence based), condoms, testing for AIDS, etc.

[10] Bork, *Ibid.*, 138-139. The two quotations are documented as being taken from Maggie Gallagher, *Enemies of Eros: How the Sexual Revolution is Killing Family, Marriage, and Sex and What We Can Do About It* (Chicago: Bonus Books, 1989), 251, 252.

Sex as Displayed in the Media

The statistics are in: "According to the 2009 Youth Risk Behavior Survey, 46% of all high school seniors have had sexual intercourse, and 14% have had 4 partners or more."[11] Studies are ongoing about the influence that media has on sexual behavior of teens, but initial reports are very much as expected: exposure to more incidents of sexual content in music, movies, television, and magazines increases the risk of engaging in early sexual intercourse.[12] The kinds of media that are influencing teens are music, R-rated teen movies, teen magazines, internet, social networking Web sites, advertisements.

> The media has become one of the leading sex educators in the United States today. While some government programs present an abstinence only sex education program, ... the media are decidedly not abstinence only. In fact, the United States has some of the most sexually suggestive media in the world. American media make sex seem like a harmless sport in which everyone engages, and results of considerable research

---

[11] Victor C. Strasburger, MD, "Sexuality, Contraception, and the Media," *Pediatrics* 126: 3 (September 1, 2010), 576-582. The statistics are documented in the article as coming from Centers for Disease Control and Prevention, Youth risk behavior surveillance: United States, 2009. *MMWR Surveill Summ. 2010;* 59 (SS-5): 1-148. Available online at *http://pediatrics.aappublications.org/content/126/3/576.full*, accessed 4/15/2014.

[12] See "Sexy Media Matter: Exposure to Sexual Content in Music, Movies, Television, and Magazines Predicts Black and White Adolescents' Sexual Behavior" by Jane D. Brown, Kelly Ladin L'Engle, Carol J. Pardun, Guang Guo, Kristin Kenneavy, and Christine Jackson (all PhDs except one who had a MA), *Pediatrics* 117: 4 (April 2006), 1018-1027. Available online at *http://pediatrics.aappublications.org/content/117/4/1018.full.pdf+html*, accessed 4/15/2014.

NOTES

_____
_____
_____
_____
_____
_____

have indicated that the media can have a major effect on young people's attitudes and behaviors. In fact, the media may function as a "superpeer" in convincing adolescents that sexual activity is a normative behavior for young teenagers. In a survey of 2100 11- to 17-year-old girls, only the 11-year-olds reported that they did not feel pressure from the media to begin having sex.[13]

How frequent is sex presented on TV? "More than half (56%) of all shows contain sexual content; these shows average more than three scenes with sex per hour. Fifty-four percent of all shows contain talk about sex, and 23% of all shows contain depictions of sexual behavior. Seven percent of all shows contain scenes in which sexual intercourse is either depicted or strongly implied. ... In the one-week sample analyzed for this study, there were 71 scenes in which intercourse was strongly implied, and 17 scenes in which intercourse was actually depicted, albeit discreetly."[14]

The undeniable fact is that our children are being bombarded by a hedonistic picture of human sexuality at worst and a secularistic viewpoint at best. Teens are watching about 22 hours of TV per week. When the amount of time listening to music is factored in, they are being immersed in a culture that makes them feel pressured to be sexually active.

Sex According to the Bible

Having described sex as it is portrayed in American culture, let us move to see what the Bible teaches about sex.

---

[13] Strasburger, *op. cit.*

[14] "Sex on TV: A Biennial Report to the Kaiser Family Foundation" by Dale Kunkel, Kirstie M. Cope, Wendy Jo Maynard Farinola, Erica Biely, Emma Rollin, and Edward Donnerstein (1999). Available online at *http://files.eric.ed.gov/fulltext/ED445371.pdf*, accessed 4/15/2014.

1. God created humans as sexual beings.
The Genesis narrative explains, "So God created man in His own image; in the image of God He created him; *male and female He created them*" (Gen. 1:27). God created mankind as sexual beings, which, as part of the creation, was pronounced "very good" (Gen. 1:31). Human sexuality is not ugly or dirty, as is frequently attributed to puritanical values.

2. Sex is for pleasure and procreation.
Sexual cohabitation was understood from the beginning as how children were born. "And Adam knew Eve his wife; and she conceived, and bare Cain" (Gen. 4:1). "To know" one's wife is an expression the Holy Spirit used to refer to sexual intercourse.[15] God's divine will was for children to be born into a family unit, reared by their biological parents. However, sex was not restricted to those times when one wished to reproduce, as Catholic doctrine teaches (but few, if any Catholics practice).[16] The wise man taught young men to avoid sexual intercourse with anyone other than one's spouse saying,

> Drink water from your own cistern,
> And running water from your own well.
> Should your fountains be dispersed abroad,

---

[15] The Hebrew word *yada'* is used in this context to mean "*know a person* carnally, of sexual intercourse" (*The Brown, Driver, and Briggs Hebrew and English Lexicon*, 394).

[16] For an online presentation of Catholic teaching on sexual morality, see *http://en.wikipedia.org/wiki/Catholic_teachings_on_sexual_morality*, accessed 4/15/2014. The Catholic teaching that cohabitation is for the purpose of conceiving children is based on this statement: "Although all three principal discussions of marriage in the New Testament (Matthew 19, I Corinthians 7, and Ephesians 5) omit any reference to generating children, later Catholic moral doctrine consistently emphasized that the only proper purpose of sexual relations was to conceive children."

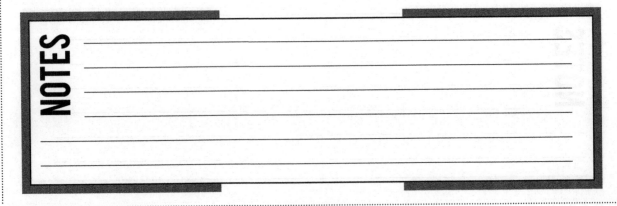

NOTES
_____
_____
_____
_____
_____
_____

Streams of water in the streets?
Let them be only your own,
And not for strangers with you.
Let your fountain be blessed,
And rejoice with the wife of your youth.
As a loving deer and a graceful doe,
Let her breasts satisfy you at all times;
And always be enraptured with her love.
For why should you, my son,
Be enraptured by an immoral woman,
And be embraced in the arms of a seductress?
(Prov. 5:15-20).

Like the passage in 1 Corinthians 7:1-5, this passage teaches that sexual gratification should be found in one's own spouse in order to avoid the temptation of sexual immorality. One should find sexual pleasure in his/her own mate, not another (cf. Song of Sol. 4:5; 7:1-9).

3. Sex is to be between two humans.
This may appear pointless to include, but the Scriptures warn against it, so I am including it. The Scriptures forbid bestiality – the unnatural sexual connection with an animal; sex with animals is also called "zoophilia" (lit., animal love). The punishment for bestiality was putting to death both the human (male or female) and the beast. "If a man mates with an animal, he shall surely be put to death, and you shall kill the animal. If a woman approaches any animal and mates with it, you shall kill the woman and the animal. They shall surely be put to death. Their blood is upon them" (Lev. 20:15-16; cf. 18:23; cf. Exod. 22:19; Deut. 27:21). If the *Wikipedia* article on "zoophilia" is accurate, the practice is ongoing in the twenty-first century.

4. Sex is to be heterosexual. The Scriptures
condemn homosexuality. "You shall not lie with a male as with a woman. It is an abomination" (Lev. 18:22). In the nation of Israel, the sin/crime was punishable by death (Lev. 20:13). The New Testament also condemns homosexuality (1 Cor. 6:9-11; Rom. 1:26-27; 1 Tim. 1:10).

5. Sex is within the bounds of marriage.
The author of Hebrews wrote, "Marriage is honorable among all, and the bed undefiled; but fornicators and adulterers God will judge" (Heb. 13:4). Indeed, withholding oneself from satisfying his mate's sexual desires not only places that person in a position of temptation, but is sinful (1 Cor. 7:1-5). Paul wrote, "Let the husband render to his wife the affection due her, and likewise also the wife to her husband. The wife does not have authority over her own body, but the husband does. And likewise the husband does not have authority over his own body, but the wife does. Do not deprive one another except with consent for a time, that you may give yourselves to fasting and prayer; and come together again so that Satan does not tempt you because of your lack of self-control" (1 Cor. 7:3-5).

6. Sex outside these boundaries is sinful.
The following are specifically condemned in Scripture: fornication (1 Cor. 6:9-20; Gal. 5:19), adultery (Gal. 5:19; Exod. 20:14; Lev. 20:10; John 8:1-11; Rom. 13:9), homosexuality (see above), bestiality (see above), rape (Deut. 22:25-27; 2 Sam. 13:1-15), incestuous relationships (sexual relationships with close relatives; see Lev. 18; 20; cf. Gen. 19:31-36; 35:22; 49:4; 2 Sam. 13:14). For whoredom and prostitution, see Bible dictionaries for more information.

Conclusion

The pluralist approach to sexuality, and all other ethical behaviors, is that ethics are situational and autonomous. The idea is that every individual determines for himself what

NOTES
_____
_____
_____
_____
_____
_____
_____

is right and wrong in a particular situation. So long as two people are in "love," sex is justified; then came along the "hook-up" where "love" has nothing to do with sex. The fact is that pluralism believes "anything goes" in sexual conduct – so long as it is consensual and does not hurt anyone. But that implies non-consensual sex and sex that hurts someone are wrong. What standard declares that those forms of sexual conduct are wrong?

American society has degraded itself by its promiscuous view of sex. Children are having babies; children are being raised in fatherless homes (which contributes to poverty, violence, and crime); sexual diseases are epidemic; adultery destroys the home. Children are being exposed to pornographic images at earlier and earlier ages. The effect this will have on future generations is frightening. The degree to which this will contribute to early rape, molestation, and assault are only beginning to be seen. Despite these obvious problems being created by this sexual behavior, America seems bent on pursuing her immoralities.

Questions

1. How were sexual deities worshiped in ancient pagan societies? _____
   _____
   _____

2. How did that influence Israel?_____
   _____
   _____

3. Explain why you agree or disagree that American has made sex a god. _____
   _____
   _____

4. What is the atheistic and modern American view of acceptable sexual behavior?_____
   _____
   _____

5. On what grounds could an atheist call any sexual behavior "evil"? _____
   _____
   _____
   _____

NOTES
_____
_____
_____
_____
_____

6. What is "recreational sex" and what is wrong with that concept of sexuality? _____
_____
_____
_____

7. How is sex depicted...

   a. On television?_____

   b. In rap music? _____

   c. In movies? _____

   d. In advertising? _____

8. How effective is TV as an educator of sexual morés? _____
_____
_____
_____

9. What are we to learn about sexuality from Genesis 1:27, 31? _____
_____
_____
_____

10. What is God's will for bringing children into the world? _____
_____
_____
_____

11. What is wrong with the Catholic doctrine that the purpose of sex is only for conception? _____
_____
_____
_____
_____

NOTES
_____
_____
_____
_____
_____

12. What passages show that sex is for one's pleasure and not limited to procreation? _____

_____

_____

_____

_____

13. What is bestiality and what does the Bible teach about the practice?_____

_____

_____

14. What verses in the Mosaic Law condemn homosexuality?_____

_____

_____

15. What verses in the New Testament condemn homosexuality? _____

_____

_____

16. How does God's limiting of sex to the marriage relationship protect His people from problems (Heb. 13:4)? _____

_____

_____

17. List several sexual sins mentioned in the Bible. _____

_____

_____

_____

_____

NOTES

_____

_____

_____

_____

_____

What Is Man?

The Bible view of man is grounded in creation. The omnipotent God created the heavens and the earth in six days. The crowning point of creation was the creation of mankind in God's own image. The text reads as follows:

> Then God said, "Let Us make man in Our image, according to Our likeness; let them have dominion over the fish of the sea, over the birds of the air, and over the cattle, over all the earth and over every creeping thing that creeps on the earth." So God created man in His own image; in the image of God He created him; male and female He created them. Then God blessed them, and God said to them, "Be fruitful and multiply; fill the earth and subdue it; have dominion over the fish of the sea, over the birds of the air, and over every living thing that moves on the earth." And God said, "See, I have given you every herb that yields seed which is on the face of all the earth, and every tree whose fruit yields seed; to you it shall be for food. Also, to every beast of the earth, to every bird of the air, and to everything that creeps on the earth, in which there is life, I have given every green herb for food"; and it was so. Then God saw everything that He had made, and indeed it was very good. So the evening and the morning were the sixth day (Gen. 1:26-31).

Although all of life proceeds from God and is dependent upon Him, the Biblical narrative places a separating wall between mankind and the rest of God's animal creation in that mankind alone is made in the image of God (Gen. 1:26-27; 5:1-3; 9:6). Because man is created in the image of God, he has dominion over animal creation (Gen. 1:28); the plant and animal creations are to be used by mankind for food (Gen. 1:28-29; 9:3-4). Reflecting on man's place in creation, the psalmist wrote,

> When I consider Your heavens, the work of Your fingers,
> The moon and the stars, which You have ordained,
> What is man that You are mindful of him,
> And the son of man that You visit him?
> For You have made him a little lower than the angels,
> And You have crowned him with glory and honor.
> You have made him to have dominion over the works of Your hands;
> You have put all things under his feet,
> All sheep and oxen –
> Even the beasts of the field,
> The birds of the air,
> And the fish of the sea
> That pass through the paths of the seas.
> O LORD, our Lord,
> How excellent is Your name in all the earth! (Psa. 8:3-9).[1]

When men reject God and develop an alternative worldview,[2] the logical implications

---

[1] This text is quoted in 1 Corinthians 15:27 and Hebrews 2:8ff.

[2] The commonality in many worldviews is their opposition to the supernatural, the refusal to recognize anything in nature, life, or history, outside the lines of natural development.

Before and After	
How does man's inhumane treatment of others relate to his concept of what man is?	
Before	**After**

and consequences affect everything that worldview touches. A worldview that eliminates God, miracles, and revelation is destined to redefine who and what man is.

This lesson will contrast the Biblical view of man with that of modern secularism. A brief history of the shift away from the Biblical view of man to the secular view is presented, followed by material to show the implications of the secularist view of man on morals and values.

The Myth of Human Progress

The Enlightenment, in the late 17th century, began a shift in thinking that reinterpreted man's role in the universe. Stanley J. Grenz said, "[T]he new science of the Age of Reason pictured the universe as a giant machine in which humans were but a small part. Human beings managed to stop thinking of themselves as creatures subservient to God, but in doing so they also dethroned themselves from their lofty position near the pinnacle of creation, exercising authority as stewards over the rest of the created order."[3] The age of Enlightenment replaced God with humanity on center stage in history.

On November 24, 1859 Charles Darwin published his book, *On the Origins of Species*, in which he laid the foundations for evolutionary biology. Though Darwin himself believed in God, his theory provided an explanation of the existing order apart from God. Over the years, God was eliminated from the model and atheistic evolution pre-dominated. The explanation for the development of the species is natural selection,

---

[3] Grenz, *A Primer on Postmodernism*, 63. Richard Weikart said that "those with a naturalistic bent often argued that Darwinism stripped humans of their special status in the cosmos" ("Darwinism and Death," 343).

or the survival of the fittest. Another key element of Darwinian thought is transmutation of species – the idea that one species can transmute into another species. In Darwinian thought, man is the product of the random evolution of living things.

Liberalism's[4] acceptance of the evolutionary theory led them to believe that mankind had not only evolved over millions of years but that he is continuing his human evolution; he is ever improving. Evolutionary theory had a sense of optimism. Some races of men were more advanced than others. Hitler and the Nazi regime used the term *übermensch* (German word for "overman, above-human, superman") to describe their idea of a biologically superior "Aryan" or Germanic master race.[5] The notion also spawned the idea that there were "inferior humans" (*untermenschen*) who could be dominated or enslaved. The Nazi's concept resulted in the systematic elimination of those they considered to be inferiors (mentally retarded, handicapped, etc.) as well as perfectly healthy members of what they labeled as inferior races (Jews). The myth of human progress based on evolutionary theory was shattered by World Wars I and II in which the most scientifically

---

[4] Liberal Christianity (18th century onward; also called "modernism") "almost immediately rejected tenets of Christianity having to do with supernaturalism and divine intervention in history" (*http://en.wikipedia.org/wiki/Liberal_Christianity*, accessed 4/17/2014).

[5] The German prefix *über* can have connotations of superiority, transcendence, excessiveness, or intensity, depending on the words to which it is prepended. *Mensch* refers to a member of the human species, rather than to a male specifically. The adjective *übermenschlich* means super-human, in the sense of beyond human strength or out of proportion to humanity (see *http://en.wikipedia.org/wiki/%C3%9Übermensch*, accessed 4/16/2014.

NOTES

_____

_____

_____

_____

_____

_____

advanced civilizations devastated one another and carried out massive war crimes. The theological response to World Wars I and II was neo-orthodoxy with a renovated doctrine of original sin, without reliance on the inspiration of Scripture.

A materialist concept of the world results in man being viewed no differently from any other animal. Some want to add that he is the most highly developed, but they have no objective measuring stick to determine who/what is more or less highly developed. For the materialist, thoughts are mere emissions of electronic impulses in response to stimulation. Since every form of life has different response to the same stimuli, what objective measuring stick can one use to determine the superiority of one response over another (be that a worm or a Harvard graduate)? Man then becomes just another animal[6] and the study of animal behavior can be used to understand human behavior.[7]

The most prevalent explanation of man from an atheistic point of view is expressed in *Humanist Manifesto I*.

FIRST: Religious humanists regard the universe as self-existing and not created.

SECOND: Humanism believes that man is a part of nature and that he has emerged as a result of a continuous process.

THIRD: Holding an organic view of life, humanists find that the traditional dualism of mind and body must be rejected.[8]

Post-modernism rejected modernism as just another subjective worldview and replaced evolutionary optimism with a spirit of pessimism.[9] Rick Wade wrote, "Postmodernism, then, leaves us without knowledge of ultimate truths, with no basis for value judgment, and with no basis for confidence in the future. In general, then, the postmodern mood is pessimistic."[10] Without God and without revelation, man is left on his own to shape and model the world as he wishes it to be.

The modern Western individual sees himself as "the maker and molder" of himself.[11] Harvey Cox said, "Urban-secular man came to town after the funeral for the religious world view had

---

[6] The ecologist view that protecting a snail darter or a spotted owl is just as important as protecting man's well-being is rooted in the view that man is no different than other animals. Since man is not an endangered species, the endangered snail darter or spotted owl's needs take precedence over man's needs.

[7] For example, through observing animal sexuality, one may conclude that expecting a man to be monogamous is unrealistic.

[8] Available online at *http://americanhumanist.org/ Humanism/Humanist_Manifesto_I*. While *Humanist Manifesto II* says, "The preciousness and dignity of the individual person is a central humanist value," there is no logical basis for the "preciousness and dignity" of the individual person any more or less than of a single dog or flea.

[9] *Humanist Manifesto II* begins by stating that events between 1933 and 1973 "make that earlier statement seem far too optimistic." In the late nineteenth century, James Orr commented, "The descent from faith in Christ has landed us in the abyss of *Pessimism*" (*The Christian View of God and the World*, 53).

[10] Rick Wade, "Worldviews, Part 2 – Comparing Postmodernism and Other Worldviews with a Christian View," available online at *http://www.probe.org/site/c. fdKEIMNsEoG/b.4224501/k.2359/Worldviews_ Part_2__Comparing_Postmodernism_and_Other_ Worldviews_with_a_Christian_View.htm#text20*, accessed 4/17/2014.

[11] Michael Babock, *Unchristian America*, 116; cf. Harvey Cox, *The Secular City*, 97 – "man takes responsibility for directing the tumultuous tendencies of his time."

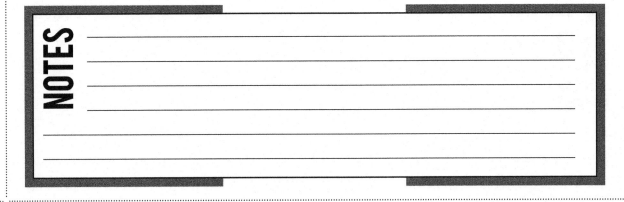

NOTES

been held. He feels no sense of deprivation and has no interest in mourning. ... In former ages, man looked to muses, gods, or 'values' for the answers to his problems. Secular man relies on himself and his colleagues for answers. He does not ask the church, the priest, or God."[12] Man only has himself in the face of bleak disasters; there is nothing better ahead of him than what has always been. Should he survive the difficult circumstances of today, he only has tomorrow filled with who knows what to face until his body ceases to function and then it terminates!

How Did Life Originate?

Modern man thinks himself intellectually superior to those who believe that God literally created the world by the power of His spoken word. Looking at existing phenomena, man tries to explain what exists based on his latest understanding of scientific knowledge. The present reigning opinion is the "Big Bang" theory.[13] The modern theories of the existence

of the universe and human life are based on theories that eliminate the supernatural. The result is this: "Life resulted from accidental chemical reactions."[14] The evolution of man is the result of fortuitous circumstances.

What then is man? Just a living being, nothing more and nothing less. Modern man sees man as part of the "circle of life" that connects all living things. In medieval times, the chain extended from God through creation; modern humanity has closed that chain into a circle that excludes God altogether. Babcock observed, "According to this radically materialistic worldview, everything we are, everything we do, and everything we think can be traced back to a common denominator, an evolutionary instinct that links all living things: the competition for food and sexual partners. The nobility that (Pico della) Mirandola still saw in humanity has been replaced by base instinct."[15]

The Value of Life Issues

What determines whether or not life is meaningful? The Darwinian doctrine of biological evolution devalued human life.[16] In the absence of God, society defines what is a person and whether or not his life is valued and meaningful. Michael Babcock wrote, "The community you are born into retains the power to confer life, personhood, and meaning on you. That doesn't bode well, of course, for the unborn

---

[12] Harvey Cox, *The Secular City*, 70.

[13] For an online summary of the "big bang theory," *see* http://en.wikipedia.org/wiki/Big_Bang. The big bang theory is based on using the present rate of expansion of the universe to measure backwards to learn what happened at the beginning, at infinity – a time when everything was infinitesimally small (the entire universe was once much smaller than a pin head) and temperature is thought to have been extremely high. At some point in the past, something happened that caused an expansion of matter – the "big bang." What is factual is that the universe is expanding at a measurable rate (though that rate depends upon the accuracy of the instruments presently being used to measure the rate of expansion and assumptions about whether that expansion rate has been constant). All else about the big bang theory is conjecture, drawn from the presuppositions of a secularist worldview (such as what is supposed to have happened in the first one-tenth of a second after the big bang).

[14] Babcock, 165.

[15] *Ibid.*, 118.

[16] See Richard Weikart, "Darwinism and Death: Devaluing Human Life in Germany 1859-1920," available online at http://www.csustan.edu/sites/default/files/History/Faculty/Weikart/Darwinism-and-Death.pdf, accessed 04/17/2014.

NOTES

child,[17] the disabled infant,[18] the inconvenient elderly person, or the suffering cancer patient.[19] When an individual's life ceases to hold any material benefit to society, then what prevents society from redesignating that individual as a nonperson? Can lives be so easily tossed away as a petty inconvenience?"[20]

The value of life issues affects life at both its beginning (abortion) and its end (euthanasia and physician assisted death). As Babcock wrote, "If one has adopted a materialistic worldview, then infanticide, suicide, and euthanasia make perfectly good sense under the right circumstances."[21] But value of life issues are not exclusively beginning and end of life issues. Value of life issues are at the center of how humans treat each other. For example, as I write, Indianapolis had a senseless killing in which a sixteen-year-old,

for no apparent reason, killed a newlywed who was out on his morning walk. Drive-by shootings are commonplace in urban America. Child abuse has not diminished since abortion on demand was justified on the grounds that it would prevent child abuse since there would be no unwanted children (as if the killing of the unborn itself was not child abuse). Child neglect constitutes about 60% of all child abuse charges. Random assaults, cases in which an assailant randomly picks a target and tries to knock him out with one punch, were regularly reported during late 2014 thru early 2015. The devaluation of human life has become so commonplace that we become numb to what is reported. The evolutionary view of human life is not spoken, but it is the same survival of the fittest that works among animals. "Nature, red in tooth and claw"[22] could well be used to describe the streets of urban America. Indeed, twenty-first century Americans place a different value on human life than Christianity does.

In the Christian system, human life is so valued that God sent His Son to die on Calvary for man's salvation (John 3:16). One should love his neighbor as he loves himself (Matt. 22:39). Indeed, some men would even lay down their lives to save the life of a friend (Rom. 5:7). The value of life is also seen in the punishment for taking life (Gen. 9:6) and in the divine requirement to alleviate the suffering of others (Matt. 25:31-46; James 1:27; Gal. 6:10). How different is the Christian view of human life than that described in the paragraph above.

---

[17] Robert H. Bork, nominee for the Supreme Court, who was "borked" by left-wing Senators, noted that "a fetus is a person only if the mother values its life" (*Slouching Toward Gomorrah*, 176).

[18] Michael Babcock relates that Peter Singer, ethicist at Princeton University, "has achieved notoriety for his view that it is ethical – and socially desirable – to euthanize disabled infants." Singer argues "that infants do not enter this world as persons; rather, they acquire personhood through 'social construction.' As such, infants have no rights, nor do they even acquire rights until society has conferred them by consensus" (*Unchristian America*, 184).

[19] Euthanasia and physician assisted death (PAD) are legal in several countries (Australia, Belgium, Columbia, Luxembourg, The Netherlands, etc.). Physician assisted death is legal in Oregon, Washington, and Vermont as of this writing (*http://en.wikipedia.org/wiki/Assisted_suicide*, accessed 4/17/2014).

[20] Babcock, *op. cit.*, 166.

[21] *Ibid.*, 186.

---

[22] The phrase is taken from Alfred Lord Tennyson's poem "In Memoriam A.H.H" in which he was reacting to the idea of evolution that was being presented in his day.

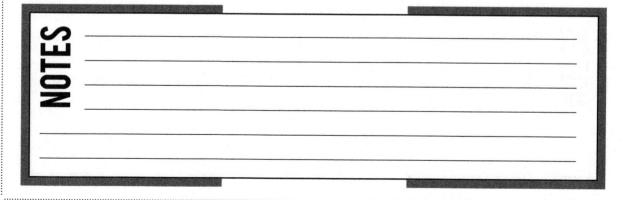

NOTES

Conclusion

The materialistic view of man devalues life at its beginning (abortion) and its end (euthanasia), as well as how we treat each other day by day.

The materialistic view of man dethrones him from his position above the rest of creation where God placed him and leaves him with a pessimistic view of life.

Questions

1. According to the Bible, what makes man unique (Gen. 1:26-27)? _____

_____

2. How does Genesis 1:26-31 distinguish man from the rest of God's animal creation? _____

_____

3. What is man's role in God's divine scheme (Gen. 1:26-31)? _____

_____

4. What astounded the author of Psalm 8:3-9? _____

_____

5. What presupposition underlies the materialistic worldview?_____

_____

6. According to Darwinian thought, how is man distinguished from other animals?_____

_____

7. How did Darwinian evolution lead to the Nazi belief that the Aryan race was superior to all others?

_____

_____

_____

8. What did Nazi's do with those they believed were inferior? _____

_____

9. How could a materialist determine that mankind is the most highly evolved of all species? _____

_____

10. Why is the modern view of man so pessimistic?_____

_____

NOTES

11. How does modern evolutionary theory think life began? _____

_____

12. What view of man would cause the ecology movement to think that it should shut down logging in a section of the country dependent upon logging for its economical survival in order to save a spotted owl? _____

_____

13. How does one determine the value of life...

    a. According to the Bible?_____

       _____

       _____

    b. According to materialistic/atheistic thought? _____

       _____

14. Why are the following morally neutral, according to atheism or materialism?

    a. Abortion _____

       _____

    b. Euthanasia or doctor assisted death _____

       _____

15. How does modern inner city crime display the devaluation of life?_____

_____

_____

_____

NOTES
_____
_____
_____
_____
_____
_____

Secular Eschatology

The word "eschatology" is derived from the Greek words *eschatos*, meaning "last," and *-logy* meaning "the study of." *Merriam-Webster* gives the word this definition:

> **1:** a branch of theology concerned with the final events in the history of the world or of humankind
>
> **2:** a belief concerning death, the end of the world, or the ultimate destiny of humankind; specifically: any of various Christian doctrines concerning the Second Coming, the resurrection of the dead, or the Last Judgment[1]

Christianity is not the only religion that has an eschatology; in fact, all religions have an eschatology whether systematically developed or not.

The design of this lesson is to make us aware of the eschatology of secularism in our society, whether that secularism is derived from agnosticism, materialism, atheism, modernism, or post-modernism. The doctrine of last things from the secular point of view will be contrasted with the Christian expectation for the future.

_____

[1] *http://www.merriam-webster.com/dictionary/eschatology.*

Secular Eschatology

The materialist or secularist view of the end of the world is not completely worked out. Some theorists think that it will all end when gravity causes the expanding universe to contract again until it all crashes together in a "Big Crunch." But that will create another super black hole that will explode in another Big Bang, creating a brand new universe — and, in effect, returning us to the cyclical notion of time. Most scientists today, though, seem to hold to linear time and the view that the universe will keep expanding forever, though at some point it will become too cold to sustain any kind of life. This view of the end times is called the "Big Freeze."[2]

For man, secularists are consistent in believing that the end of physical life is the end of a person's existence. Writing in 1893, James Orr spoke of the materialist or atheistic view of man, "It is a significant circumstance that the modern unbelieving view of the world has no

_____

[2] *http://www.ligonier.org/learn/articles/secular-eschatology/*; cf. *http://en.wikipedia.org/wiki/Big_Crunch* and *http://en.wikipedia.org/wiki/Future_of_an_expanding_universe.*

Before and After	
What is going on?	
You went to a funeral that had secular music, people told humorous stories about their loved one and explained that he would live forever in their memory. They asked you to pass at the end and reflect on the influence of his life on you.	
Before	**After**

hope to give us of a life beyond the grave."[3] What does atheism have to offer in place of the Christian hope of everlasting life? Orr continued, "The hope proposed to us in lieu of individual immortality is that of 'corporate immortality,' the privilege of joining the 'choir invisible' of those who have laboured in the service of humanity, though they live now only in the grateful memory of posterity."[4] That Orr correctly understood the consequences of atheism is confirmed by the following quotations.

Humanist Manifesto II emphatically asserts the following:

SECOND: Promises of immortal salvation or fear of eternal damnation are both illusory and harmful. They distract humans from present concerns, from self-actualization, and from rectifying social injustices. Modern science discredits such historic concepts as the "ghost in the machine" and the "separable soul." Rather, science affirms that the human species is an emergence from natural evolutionary forces. As far as we know, the total personality is a function of the biological organism transacting in a social and cultural context. There is no credible evidence that life survives the death of the body. We continue to exist in our progeny and in the way that our lives have influenced others in our culture.[5]

Writing in *A Secular Humanist Declaration*, Paul Kurtz said,

While religions have no doubt offered comfort to the bereaved and dying by holding forth the

promise of an immortal life, they have also aroused morbid fear and dread. We have found no convincing evidence that there is a separable "soul" or that it exists before birth or survives death. We must therefore conclude that the ethical life can be lived without the illusions of immortality or reincarnation.[6]

What is left for the humanist/atheist/materialist? D. A. Carson quoted from one of the novels of John Fowles, *The Magus*,[7] spoken when the character had learned that his girlfriend had died. The character spoke as follows:

Staring out to sea, I finally forced myself to stop thinking of her as someone still somewhere ... but as a shovelful of ashes already scattered, as a broken link, a biological dead end, an eternal withdrawal from reality, a once complex object that now dwindled, dwindled, left nothing behind except a smudge like a fallen speck of soot on a blank sheet of paper. ... I did not cry for her ... but I sat in the silence of that night, that infinite hostility to man, to permanence, to love, remembering her, remembering her.[8]

As a preacher, I ask myself, "How would you like to say such words at someone's funeral?" How much comfort does atheism have to offer in the hour of death?

In 1978, I attended a discussion between atheist Madelyn Murray O'Hair and evangelist Gaston Cogdell. Mrs. O'Hair's husband, Richard O'Hair, had recently died.[9] As Cogdell began

---

[3] James Orr, *The Christian View of God and the World*, 151.

[4] *Ibid.*

[5] *Humanist Manifesto II* is available online at *http://americanhumanist.org/Humanism/Humanist_Manifesto_II*, accessed 4/18/2014.

[6] Kurtz, *A Secular Humanist Declaration*, 19.

[7] John Fowles, *The Magus*, 2nd edition (London: Jonathan Cape, 1977), 441.

[8] Carson, *The Gagging of God*, 207.

[9] Mrs. O'Hair had married Richard O'Hair, a former U.S. Marine, in 1965. Although the marriage resulted in separation, she remained married to him until his death in 1978.

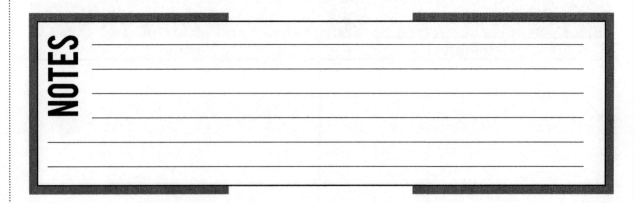

NOTES
_____
_____
_____
_____
_____
_____

his address to the audience, he expressed his condolences to Mrs. O'Hair at the recent "passing" of her husband. Although this is not a direct quotation, her response in essence was this: "Gaston, my husband did not 'pass' anywhere. He terminated!" This is the atheist view of death.

Human Accountability

How should one live, given the atheist view that life on earth is all that there is? If one has the ability to forcibly take from others whatever he wants for himself, without suffering temporal consequences (imprisonment, retaliation, etc.), why shouldn't he do that? If sexual indulgence gives man pleasure, why should he care what impact the sexual encounter has on his consort? Perhaps he pays her for her "services" and she accepts the "risks" (pregnancy, disease, etc.). Perhaps he lies to her to get what he wants and she naively believes his lies. Given the humanist view of life's end – there is no accountability after death, why shouldn't he do this?

There is a sense in which the atheist view of death is comforting, at least theoretically. It releases man from accountability for his deeds on earth and the fear of eternal damnation. At the same time, the atheist view of death also takes away any comfort that one's loved one continues to exist after this life, that his body will be raised from the tomb, and that he will live endlessly in a place of peace and rest. Without this hope, one motive for righteous living has been removed.

A Secular Funeral

As the secular worldview permeates American culture, funerals have changed. Funerals used to be highlighted by a gospel sermon that encouraged the audience to prepare for God's day of judgment. Preachers exhorted the audience to look at their relationship with God in view of a coming judgment. Such lessons obviously made those who were content in their sins uncomfortable.

As liberal religion rejected the divine inspiration of Scripture and lost faith in God's promises of eternal punishment of the wicked, funeral sermons changed. Today, preachers typically leave the impression that everyone has reason to hope for everlasting life, regardless of how he lived. Their homilies are, therefore, non-offensive and reassuring to those in the audience; unfortunately, their funeral orations leave the audiences thinking they can continue living as they are without fear of eternal damnation. Today's funeral speech is expected to say good words about the dead and comfort those who mourn his loss with the reassurance that all will share eternal salvation.

The secularism that is rife in modern culture has Americans trending toward secular funerals – funerals that use secular music, consist of tributes and the telling humorous anecdotes from the individual's life by the family and friends. The service may begin and end without a single reference to God, heaven and hell, judgment day, etc. Without faith in the eternal nature of the soul and the resurrection of the dead, the modern "comforting" message is something like this: "He will live forever in our memory,"[10] "As long as memory endures, his influence will be felt," or "Each of you take a moment of

---

[10] As if the mind never forgets. As one ages, he frequently has trouble recalling the names of an individual whom he has known many years. If one walks through a cemetery, he can see weather-worn grave markers that are so eroded that one cannot determine whose name is on the marker. Obviously, that person has passed from all human memory.

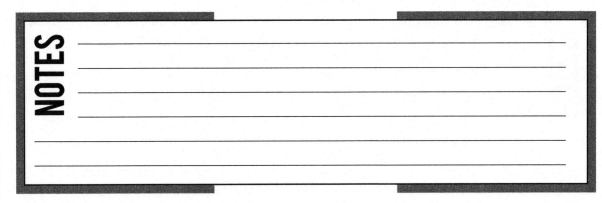
NOTES

silent meditation, and think of his influence and contemplate the many joys he experienced in his life, and how privileged he was to live, love, and be loved by those gathered here." The speaker(s) may recount the things the deceased enjoyed: book clubs, service organizations, professional life, recreational activities, travel, music, and movies, etc.

The bottom line of secular eschatology is this: when the last breath of life is breathed, the individual ceases to exist. There is nothing beyond death. There is no resurrection and no reincarnation – no hope! In a letter to Lowes Dickinson, Bertrand Russell (1872-1970), well-known agnostic or atheist, wrote: "We stand on the shores of an ocean, crying to the night and the emptiness; sometimes a voice answers out of the darkness. But it is a voice of one drowning; and in a moment the silence returns" (Bertrand Russell, *Autobiography*, p. 287 as quoted by Leroy Koopman, "Famous Atheists Give Their Testimonies," *Moody Monthly*, November 1975, p. 124).[11]

The agnostic Robert Green Ingersoll (1833-1899) spoke at his brother's (Ebon C. Ingersoll) funeral saying,

Life is a narrow vale between the cold and barren peaks of two eternities. We strive in vain to look beyond the heights. We cry aloud, and the only answer is the echo of our wailing cry. From the voiceless lips of the unreplying dead there comes no word; but in the night of death hope sees a star, and listening love can hear the rustle of a wing. He who sleeps here, when dying, mistaking the approach of death for the return of health, whispered with his last breath: "I am better now." Let us believe, in spite of doubts

and dogmas, and tears and fears, that these dear words are true of all the countless dead.[12]

Such hopeless words! Contrast these words with Paul's words in the face of death:

Behold, I tell you a mystery: We shall not all sleep, but we shall all be changed-- in a moment, in the twinkling of an eye, at the last trumpet. For the trumpet will sound, and the dead will be raised incorruptible, and we shall be changed. For this corruptible must put on incorruption, and this mortal must put on immortality. So when this corruptible has put on incorruption, and this mortal has put on immortality, then shall be brought to pass the saying that is written: "Death is swallowed up in victory." "O Death, where is your sting? O Hades, where is your victory?" The sting of death is sin, and the strength of sin is the law. But thanks be to God, who gives us the victory through our Lord Jesus Christ (1 Cor. 15:51-57).

Christian Eschatology

Although it should be familiar to most who are reading this, it is beneficial to be reminded of what lies ahead. Eschatology can be studied from two points of view: (1) When a person experiences death and (2) When the end of the world occurs.

1. When a person experiences death. The Scriptures teach that the soul survives the death of the body (Eccl. 12:7; Luke 23:42-43; 2 Cor. 5:1-11; Phil. 1:23). The clearest presentation of what happens at death is found in Luke 16:19-31. At death, the body is buried, but the spirit continues to exist (cf. Rev. 6:9-11; 7:9, 14; 20:4). The righteous spirits are in a place

---

[11] Taken from *http://www.conservapedia.com/ Hopelessness_of_atheism*, accessed 4/21/2014.

[12] Quotation is taken from James D. Bales, *Man on All Fours*, 86. The speech from which the quotation is taken is also available online at *http://www.bartleby. com/268/10/9.html*, accessed 4/21/2014).

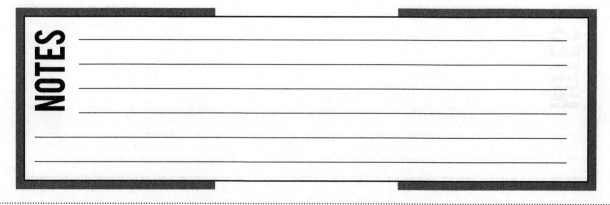

NOTES

called "Paradise" (Luke 23:42-43) or "Abraham's bosom" (Luke 16:22) and the wicked are in a placed called torment (Luke 16:23; cf. 2 Pet. 2:4; Jude 6). There the soul awaits the second coming and judgment at which time it will be reunited with the resurrected body.

2. At the end of the world these following events will occur: (a) The trumpet shall sound (1 Cor. 15:52; 1 Thess. 4:16); (b) The Lord will descend from heaven (1 Thess. 4:16; Acts 1:11); (c) The dead, both righteous and wicked, will be raised in a body fitted for eternity (John 5:28-29; 1 Cor. 15:42-49); (d) The living will be transformed into a body fitted for eternity (1 Cor. 15:52-57; 1 Thess. 4:17); (e) The physical earth will be burned up (2 Pet. 3:10; cf. Psa. 102:26; Isa. 51:6; Heb. 1:11; Rev. 20:11; 21:1); (f) Judgment will occur (Matt. 25:31-46; Acts 17:30-31; 2 Cor. 5:10; Rom. 14:12); (g) The righteous will go into everlasting life (Matt. 25:46; John 5:28-29; Rev. 7:15-17; 21:1–22:5); (h) The wicked will be cast into eternal damnation, which is eternal death (John 5:28-29; Rev. 20:11-15; 21:8; Rom. 2:8-9).

As one looks at Christian eschatology, in contrast to the eschatology of secularism, he sees these differences:

Christian eschatology holds mankind responsible for his conduct on earth, whereas secularism's eschatology has no final retribution for evil committed against others. Adolf Hitler, whose social policies led to the death of over 6,000,000 Jews in the Holocaust, suffers no more or less than one of those Jews whom he put to death in the gas chambers. Hitler had the same fate as the peerless Apostle Paul, according to secularism – physical death. On the other hand, Christian eschatology says that Adolf Hitler will stand before God and give account to God for every deed he did while in the body (2 Cor. 5:10; Matt. 25:31-32; Rom. 2:6; 14:10; Gal. 6:7; Eph. 6:8; Col. 3:24-25; Rev. 22:12), every idle word he spoke (Matt. 12:36-37) and every thought of his evil heart (Heb. 4:12-13). What is true of Hitler is true of every man: he must stand before the judgment seat of Christ to give answer for his deeds, words, and thoughts. The judgment is a motivation to live righteously:

> Therefore, since all these things will be dissolved, what manner of persons ought you to be in holy conduct and godliness, looking for and hastening the coming of the day of God, because of which the heavens will be dissolved, being on fire, and the elements will melt with fervent heat? Nevertheless we, according to His promise, look for new heavens and a new earth in which righteousness dwells. Therefore, beloved, looking forward to these things, be diligent to be found by Him in peace, without spot and blameless; and consider that the longsuffering of our Lord is salvation – as also our beloved brother Paul, according to the wisdom given to him, has written to you (2 Pet. 3:11-15).

Christian eschatology gives purpose to life. Man's purpose is to give glory to God (Rom. 11:36; 1 Cor. 10:31; Col. 1:16; Eccl. 12:13). Man's obligation is to present himself as a living sacrifice to God (Rom. 12:1). God is sometimes most gloriously praised when suffering man continues serving God. Think of the examples of such saints: (a) Joseph (Gen. 37-50); (b) Job; (c) Paul (2 Tim. 4:6-8); (d) the heroes of faith in Hebrews 11; etc. Throughout the ages, suffering saints have endured hardships, and sometimes death, in order to serve their Lord. The three Hebrew children, Shadrach, Meshach, and Abed-nego, determined that it is better to die in obedience to God than to live in disobedience to him (Dan. 3). Consequently, they refused to bow

NOTES

_____

_____

_____

_____

_____

_____

before the King's idol, choosing certain death rather than to disobey God. The Apostles chose to suffer a beating rather than cease preaching salvation through Jesus Christ (Acts 4:19; 5:29, 40-41). These saints understood what life's true purpose is.

Christian eschatology gives meaning to history. When God and His will are eliminated from man's worldview, history is meaningless. The events of life are happenstance events moving toward absolutely no goal. The Christian faith gives meaning to history. Herbert Schlossberg wrote,

> Modern people seriously considering the meaning of history generally conclude either that it has no meaning – "just one ... (profanity omitted, mw) thing after another" or a more sophisticated equivalent – or that it contains within itself its own principle of teleology, what we have referred to as the historicist fallacy. The Christian faith that once informed Western society had an answer that was different from either, but people who rejected that faith naturally rejected the interpretation of history that was an integral part of it. The biblical view is that history had a beginning and will have an end, and that both the beginning and the end are in God's hands. Therefore, what comes between them is invested with meaning and purpose... .[13]

In the absence of a biblical purpose, "history is devoid of meaning and purpose."[14] Schlossberg quotes Herman Dooyeweerd (*In the Twilight of Western Thought: Studies in the Pretended Autonomy of Philosophical Thought,* 63) to say, "History has no windows looking out into eternity. Man is completely enclosed in it and cannot elevate himself to a supra-historical level of contemplation. History is the be-all and end-all of man's existence and of his faculty of experience.

---

[13] Schlossberg, *Idols of Destruction*, 27.

[14] *Ibid.*, 24.

And it is ruled by destiny, the inescapable fate."[15] The meaninglessness of history contributes to one's pessimistic belief that life is meaningless. However, God's eternal and providential will and purpose give meaning to history.

Christian eschatology offers mankind hope. Atheism may be satisfying to the human spirit when glorious days are present, he is enjoying his prosperity, and forgetting about his God (Deut. 8:10-18). However, there are no words from the atheistic, secularist, or agnostic philosophers that comfort one's heart when one's mate of fifty years passes, when one loses a child because a drunk driver slammed into his bicycle, when cancer takes the life of a mother, or some unforeseen tragedy kills one's best friend.

Christian eschatology is rooted in historical events. Why should one believe that he will one day be raised from the dead? Because Christ is the first fruits of the resurrection and, as first fruits, the guarantee of others to come (1 Cor. 15:20-24). Why should one think that there is going to be a judgment day? Because God gave assurance thereof by the resurrection of Jesus from the dead (Acts 17:30-31). Christian eschatology is not grounded in the whimsical notions of fantasy; it is grounded in the reality of Jesus's resurrection, ascension into heaven, and second coming.

Conclusion

Humanists belittle the Christian hope. *Humanist Manifesto II* says, "Salvationism, based on mere affirmation, still appears as harmful, diverting people with false hopes of heaven hereafter."[16] Again, "Promises of immortal

---

[15] Schlossberg, *op. cit.,* 14-15.

[16] Available online at *http://americanhumanist. org/Humanism/Humanist_Manifesto_II*, accessed

NOTES

salvation or fear of eternal damnation are both illusory and harmful."[17] However, humanists have nothing but death, understood as the termination of one's existence, to put in place of Christian hope. They have no reason to go on living when the number of life's pleasant moments are far outweighed by misery. Suicide and euthanasia are viewed as better options in such circumstances.

Christianity, however, has promise, not only for the life that now is, but also for the life to come (1 Tim. 4:8). The Christian ethical system provides guidance for the most enriching earthly life as well as the hope for eternal life in the world to come.

The two options – secularism and Christianity – are before you. Which will you choose?

4/22/2014.

[17] *Ibid.*

Questions

1. What is "eschatology"? _____
_____
_____

2. What happens at death, from the secular (atheist) point of view? _____
_____
_____

3. Given the secular/atheist views of death, how should one live...

   a. In prosperous days? _____
   _____

   b. When suffering outweighs joy? _____
   _____

   c. When in poverty? _____
   _____

   d. When he wishes to indulge himself (in whatever pleasure)? _____
   _____

4. How do secularists seek to immortalize their deceased loved ones at a funeral service? _____
_____
_____

NOTES

_____
_____
_____
_____
_____
_____

5. How are funerals today different from those of your youth? _____
_____

6. What is the Christian view of what happens at death? _____
_____
_____

7. What is placed in the ground at death (1 Cor. 15:42-44)? _____
_____
_____

8. What is raised up at the resurrection (1 Cor. 15:42-44)? _____
_____
_____

9. What is the sequence of events that will occur at the end of time?

    a. _____

    b. _____

    c. _____

    d. _____

    e. _____

    f. _____

    g. _____

    h. _____

10. Why is human accountability for one's life...

    a. Necessary?_____

    b. Good?_____

    c. Just? _____

11. How does human accountability affect how one lives (2 Pet. 3:11-15)? _____
_____
_____

12. What is man's purpose for living...

    a. According to a Christian? _____

    b. According to an atheist?_____

13. What meaning is found in the daily events of life – history – according to...

    a. A Christian? _____

    b. An atheist? _____

14. What hope does Christianity give to mankind? _____
_____
_____

15. On what grounds does one have reason to expect resurrection and eternal life (Acts 17:30-31)?
_____
_____

Bibliography

Babcock, Michael. *Unchristian America.* Carol Stream, IL: Salt River Publishing, a division of Tyndale House Publishers, Inc., 2008.

Bales, James D. *Man on All Fours.* Search, AR: Harding College, 1973.

Bennett, William J. *The Index of Leading Cultural Indicators: American Society at the End of the Twentieth Century.* New York: Broadway Books, 1999.

Berg, Thomas C. "Religious Choice and Exclusions of Religion," *University of St. Thomas (Minnesota) School of Law, Legal Studies Research Paper Series*, PENNumbra (forthcoming 2008), 1-18.

Bork, Robert H. *Slouching Toward Gomorrah.* New York: Regan Books, 1996.

Carson, D. A. *Christ and Culture Revisited.* Grand Rapids: William B. Eerdmans Publishing Company, 2008.

_____ . *The Gagging of God: Christianity Confronts Pluralism.* Grand Rapids: Zondervan, 1996.

_____ . *The Intolerance of Tolerance.* Grand Rapids: William B. Eerdmans Publishing Company, 2012.

Cox, Harvey. *The Secular City.* New York City: The MacMillan Company, 1966 edition.

de Beauvoir, Simone. *The Second Sex.* New York: Vintage Books, 1952.

Dewey, John. *A Common Faith.* New Haven: Yale University Press, 2013. Available online at *http://yalepress.yale.edu/yupbooks/excerpts/Dewey_excerpt.pdf*, accessed 3/28/2014.

_____ . "My Pedagogic Creed," *School Journal* 54 (January 1897), 77-80. Available online at *http://dewey.pragmatism.org/creed.htm*, accessed 3/28/2014.

Fletcher, Joseph. *Situation Ethics.* Philadephia: Westminster Press, 1966.

Gaede, S. D. *When Tolerance Is No Virtue.* Downers Grove: InterVarsity Press, 1993.

Grenz, Stanley J. *A Primer on Postmodernism.* Grand Rapids: Wm. B. Eerdmans Publishing Company, 1996.

Ham, Ken and Britt Beemer. *Already Gone.* Green Forest, AR: Master Books, 2011 edition.

Ham, Ken and Greg Hall. *Already Compromised.* Green Forest, AR: Master Books, 2011.

Hernandez, Donald J. *Double Jeopardy: How Third-Grade Reading Skills and Poverty Influence High School Graduation.* April 2011 report supported by the Annie E. Casey Foundation and by the Center for Demographic Analysis, University of Albany, State University of New York. Available online at *http://files.eric.ed.gov/fulltext/ED518818.pdf*, accessed 3/31/2014.

Hughes, Richard T. *Reviving the Ancient Faith.* Grand Rapids: Wm. B. Eerdmans Publishing Co., 1996.

Humanist Manifesto I, II, III. Available from *americanhumanist.org*.

Josephus, Flavius. *The Complete Works of Josephus.* Translated by William Whiston. Grand Rapids: Kregel, 1981 edition.

Kurtz, Paul. *A Secular Humanist Declaration. Free Enquiry* I: 1 (Winter, 1980).

McConnell, "Religious Participation in Public Programs: Religious Freedom at a Crossroads," *University of Chicago Law Review* (Winter, 1992), 115-194.

McDowell, Josh and Bob Hostetler. *The New Tolerance.* Wheaton: Tyndale House, 1998.

Orr, James. *The Christian View of God and the World.* New York: Charles Scribner's Sons, 1893, third edition 1897.

Perry, Michael J. "Why Political Reliance on Religiously Grounded Morality Does Not Violate the Establishment Clause," *William and Mary Law Review* 42: 3, art. 3, pp. 663-683.

Potter, Charles Francis. *Humanizing Religion.* New York: Harper & Brothers Publishers, 1933.

Pybas, Kevin. "Religious Groups in a Free Society," presented at the Paul B. Henry Institute Symposium on Religion and Politics at Calvin College, April 23-25, 2009.

Schlossberg, Herbert. *Idols For Destruction.* Wheaton, IL: Crossway Books, 1990.

Strauss, David Friedrich. *The Life of Jesus Critically Examined.* Mifflintown, PA: Sigler Press, 2002 edition.

Sullivan, Kathleen M. "The New Religion and the Constitution," *Harvard Law Review*, 1397 (2003).

_____ . "Religion and Liberal Democracy," *University of Chicago Law Review* 59 (Winter, 1992), 195-223.

Taylor, Daniel. "Are You Tolerant? (Should you be?)" *Christianity Today* 41:1 (January 11, 1999), 43.

Tebbe, Nelson. "Excluding Religion," *University of Pennsylvania Law Review* (May, 2008), 1264-1339.

Weber, Max. *The Sociology of Religion.* Boston: Beacon Press, 1964.

Weikart, Richard. "Darwinism and Death: Devaluing Human Life in Germany 1859-1920." Available online at *http://www.csustan.edu/sites/default/files/History/Faculty/Weikart/Darwinism-and-Death.pdf*, accessed 04/17/2014.

Willis, Mike. "Build Strong Homes," *Build Strong Homes.* Edited by Mike Willis. Athens, AL: Guardian of Truth Publications, 2013.

NOTES